Mediterranean Diet Meal Plan

The Beginners Complete Guide with Meal Prep
for Weight Loss Solution, Gain Energy and Fat
Burn with Recipes.
Cookbook Secrets for Health Watchers

Table of Contents

CHAPTER 6: CULTIVATION   171

CONCLUSION   181

original author of this work can be in any fashion deemed liable for any hardship or damages that may befall them after undertaking information described herein.

Additionally, the information in the following pages is intended only for informational purposes and should thus be thought of as universal. As befitting its nature, it is presented without assurance regarding its prolonged validity or interim quality. Trademarks that are mentioned are done without written consent and can in no way be considered an endorsement from the trademark holder.

Introduction

The Mediterranean basin is the cradle of civilization – Rome and its glory, Greece in its grandeur, wizened old Egypt and the Levant. These great conquerors and statesman treaded across the world with their accomplishments, and the imprint left in our collective conscious is still greater. King Tutankhamen, Pythagoras, and Julius Caesar are names known to all, with Pythagoras earning the ire of middle schoolers the world over with his triangle math. But with their culture and influence, they also brought a second very distinct item – their food. The Mediterranean is also the home to one of the healthiest diets in the world, the creatively-named Mediterranean diet. In 2010, it received the accolade of UNESCO's World Heritage designation, placing it in a pantheon of cultural monoliths like Stonehenge and the Acropolis.

When the Romans stomped across all known civilization and beyond, to the lands that would support it, they brought three crops vital to Roman and wider Mediterranean civilization namely the grape, wheat, and the olive. Obviously, they didn't bring them everywhere - the marshy swamps of yet-mature Germany wouldn't work, nor remote and rocky Britain, but theirs. The Greek and Phoenician influence are why all the land that touches the Mediterranean is known for its bountiful and flavorful varieties of bread, olive oil, and wine. There's one more essential component, however.

You may have noticed a few things in your life – one that the Mediterranean is an ocean, and oceans are made of water, and fish – get this – live in water. The piece of our dietary puzzle? Fish. These people ate tons of it. Romans made a sauce of fermented anchovies that Italians still make to this day. Such was the depth of their devotion to consuming this animal. Fish was plentiful for them, and its incredible health benefits are what really seal this diet in as a potent tool for improving health.

This book attempts to give you a thorough tour of the Mediterranean diet; a more in-depth look at its history, health benefits, and some recipes to get you started.

Chapter 1: What is the Mediterranean Diet?

If you want to follow a diet, you may have to know what it is. Imagine that! The Mediterranean diet has been gaining notoriety in the health and nutrition world from the 1990s on, and admittedly, the term "Mediterranean diet" is vague, because any random person who lived in that part of the world technically has a Mediterranean diet. It's a fairly loose term – it's not like everyone in the Mediterranean just eats the same bread, but they all share commonalities, commonalities that have lead to reduced obesity rates and a lower chance of both heart attack and diabetes than Americans, so there's definitely something to consider here.

The Mediterranean diet is not just what people eat in the Mediterranean now; I'm sure we could scrounge up a dozen Spaniards, Algerians, and Greeks with horrible diets. Rather, the diet was devised by trying to replicate the cuisine and staples of southern Italy and Greece, the "peasant people," who ate what was local and was cheap in the 1960s. And what was local and what was cheap were the crops and foods that naturally flourish in the Mediterranean basin. As mentioned in the introduction, the principal components are wheat for making bread and pasta, grapes for wine, the olive for its nutritious oil, and although this is not a crop, we'll count it anyway, fish and other seafood. Altogether, these foods are known for their powerful ability to modulate health and are full of good fats, fiber, protein, and antioxidants.

It's significant enough to say too that most Mediterranean meals are very high in fresh vegetables, so while they aren't a "staple" of the diet - they are not up on Mount Olympus with the rest of the Mediterranean triad, but they are still very prevalent in almost all dishes. The Mediterranean is a notably fertile land and most people made a living in the old days as farmers. A combination of a knowledgeable worker base and good land made tilling dozens of varieties of fruits and vegetables very easy. Keep in mind as well that these people were the rural poor – peasants, farmers, that sort of thing. Vegetables were cheap and abundant, so that was just more encouragement to fill up on the broccoli and asparagus.

The Mediterranean is also the crossing point of many different cultures – the obvious Greco-Roman, Spanish, southern French, and all those come to mind, but it's also been a place where cultures have collided and mixed to yield a fantastic diversity of ingredients. Arabs from North Africa left their mark on the European side of the Mediterranean and vice versa. Germans and other northern Europeans came and brought more meat-based dishes and heavier use of butter to the region. All these foods came and mixed and mingled with the more native cuisine and the result is what we know today, one of the most popular cuisines in the world.

The natives of this region have been eating this food for millennia, ever since the Phoenicians first brought literacy to the Greeks, who were probably the equivalent of spear-throwing cave people to them. But even if many of them couldn't read or write, you'll find that the ancients still had their way of admonishing their foods—frescoes are being dug up constantly in Italy and Greece of people holding jugs of olive oil, bottles of wine, and the like. A recent find in Antioch, modern-day Turkey, shows a skeleton reclining with a jug of wine and a loaf of bread and the caption "be cheerful, enjoy your life." Clearly, even back then, these people knew how to live. Analysis of old tombs corroborates this information, wherein remains of old dried wine and olive oil gone to Hades along with the fellow in the crypt has been found. Ancient bread that still manages to be easier to chew than week-old French bread lies in wait to be used as a building material, or interestingly, as a paperweight.

Furthermore, if one actually goes through the process of looking through an old Greek or Roman cookbook, you'll find that while the recipes are different – much more bizarre to our modern palate –at the end of the day, many of the ingredients are the same, barring things like spices and new world fruits and vegetables. Cato, the Elder, would go on and on like a madman about the health benefits of cabbage, considering it most supreme of all the vegetables for medicinal purposes. The Roman legionaries even had what we might call antiquity's Gatorade – posca, which was spiced water with a touch of honey, and a splash of wine that was turned to vinegar – that kept them fighting despite the harsh conditions they had to suffer through. The same is true as you progress through the years with medieval cookbooks and even up to the early modern period, but the point is that this is a very old diet that's been nourishing people probably since before recorded history.

What's the Fuss?

What is the fuss? A question I ask myself on many occasions of many diets – but there are some interesting things to note about the health effects of this diet that really make you think.

The diet was first devised in the 1960s and was the culmination of years of nutritional study by a "couple" of researchers, - physiologist Ancel Keys, and his wife, chemist Margaret Keys, who made some very interesting findings when studying the populations of Italy and Greece. A finding which presented a paradox relative to the usual logic of nutritional reasoning of the modern western world – the classic "If you eat a lot of fat, you'll get fat, and eventually, it'll flood your arteries and they'll resemble a fast-food grease trap more than functioning tissues." To be fair, this is an easy mistake to make; calling a major macronutrient group "fat," one of the most feared adjectives in the English language, is a poor marketing decision. What they found was that the populations of these countries actually had far lower rates of heart disease than Americans then and certainly Americans now and modern research shows that the diet also has some power to mitigate the effects of other chronic lifestyle diseases, such as diabetes and cancer.

The American diet needs of a serious intervention and his svelte and trim buddy from the Mediterranean may be one of his best advisors. Americans and rural Mediterranean people, on average, have high-fat diets. Americans – we have a reputation for gorging ourselves on fast food and abominations like deep-fried butter. While this is not true of everyone, not even most people, it's a pervasive enough idea to have entered popular culture. Countries ate, on average, twice as much fat as Americans, but their rate of heart disease was significantly lower. The problem lies in the fact that Americans eat more processed trans fats as well as saturated fat, which are cheap to manufacture and kept for a long time, than other first world nations. Saturated fat is not necessarily bad for you, but that contentions on both ends are still being debated by nutritionists. Trans fat, on the other hand, has been undeniably linked to incidents of heart disease and metabolic syndrome, which is essentially diabetes before it comes into its own. Americans also recently came out of a dietary crisis that still gives us uncomfortable flashbacks. Our doctors prescribed carbohydrates to us to defend us against heart disease, and it backfired as our weight collectively ballooned out of control and heart disease may as well have stalked the street in a kill gang. It's just a simple fact that for Americans and a large portion of the modern west, some of the quickest to get foods are a simple carbohydrate, capable of both sending you flying past your caloric intake for the day and denying your feelings of satiety.

The fact is that Mediterranean people, like the French, consume as much or possibly more fat than Americans. Where the people of the Mediterranean have it right is in the type of fat they consume - mostly monounsaturated fat from olive oil and healthy saturated fats from oily fish. The humble and fantastic-smelling sardine comes to mind immediately. Finally, while the Mediterranean diet is high in carbohydrates, which has done many people no favors, it's important to remember where this diet came from, socio-economically. This is the diet of the working, rural poor. A hearty stock of people who made their living toiling in fields, the carbohydrates supplied them with the energy they needed to keep going. As a general maxim, carbohydrates are only as harmful as your lack of activity – less energy expenditure, the harder that bowl of pasta is going to hit you.

Olive oil has long been touted as a champion of health; its knockout power comes from its monounsaturated fat content and vitamin E. Monounsaturated fat has been related to dropping low-density lipoprotein (LDL "bad" cholesterol") and total cholesterol levels, which assuages the stress on the cardiovascular vessels, lessening chances of coronary heart disease. Oftentimes, it's stated that the main bearer of the health-bringing effects of the diet is the olive oil, but that really is just the tip of the iceberg.

Fish is the main animal protein eaten in a Mediterranean diet, and the fat of these oily fish is high in omega-3 fatty acids, which we seem to find more and more good things about the more time goes on. It fights heart disease, reduces global inflammation, is good for your eyes, keeps your brain in shape, and protects your epithelial tissue – your skin, hair, nails. So when people ask you how you still look so young even though your second century of life is fast approaching, you can tell them your secret isn't, in fact, vampirism, but instead, it's a diet high in omega-3 fatty acids.

An interesting thing to consider is that while omega-3s are very important for health, so are omega-6s. The problem is, on a western diet, you get plenty of omega-6s. What you're aiming for is a 1:1 ratio of omega-3s to omega-6s, what most people are closer to having is a 1:10 or 1:20, so they have 10 to 20 times as much omega-6 as omega-3.

An interesting find was reported that shows that people in two places in the world – the Okinawan islands off the coast of Japan and the island of Sardinia, in the center of the Mediterranean, have the longest-lived people on the planet, with more centenarians, nonagenarians, and octogenarians than anywhere else. Scientists have been scratching their head to figure out why;

doubtless, the answer is far more complicated than it would appear, but diet undoubtedly plays a huge part. Both the gentry of Sardinia and the people of Okinawa are known for their higher-than-average consumption of seafood, with Okinawans eating more algae and seaweed and Sardinians fonder of "traditional" seafood. Both food sources are rich in omega-3s, which corroborates what many anti-aging scientists believe about the compound. In addition, Sardinians typically follow the Mediterranean diet to a T. So, while you may not live to 100, eating like the Sardinians certainly would help.

The Mediterranean is also famed as the birthplace, top producer, and, as a whole, consumer of red wine. Red wine has come stumbling with a red-stained shirt onto the forefront of health recently, and while it's not fully elucidated if it's just red wine or all incarnations of booze, antioxidants in the wine, resveratrol being the most famous, have shown connections to better-functioning heart. Alcohol itself, in moderate quantities, shows similar benefits. The wine has a smattering of other benefits. There have been finds regarding bone mineral density, brain function, stroke prevention via thinned blood, and cancer-fighting agents.

There's also some value in saying that the diet also emphasizes whole foods over processed foods, which is always the marker of a good diet. The dairy products are usually things like cheeses and yogurts – foods that have been keeping people running for thousands of years and contains less lactose than regular milk, the main thing people have a problem digesting. Roman legionaries munched on pecorino cheese, and they conquered half of Europe on foot. Bread, which has gotten a bad rap in recent years, can be perfectly healthy if you aren't filling up on it and keep an active lifestyle. And should you make it at home, which surely many of the poorer people of the rural Mediterranean do, you know exactly what's in it as well. Lots of fresh produce, besides the more obvious benefits of vitamins and minerals, are also filled with fiber, which does wonders for both satiety and the functioning of the heart. Vegetables, along with fruit and wine, are packed full of polyphenols, a powerful anti-inflammatory from plants and plant products. A diet with a high nutrient density like that, with everything from abundant protein and fatty acids to high fiber, and a lack of pre-prepared, processed, and fast foods, means that your body, from your brain to your heart to your liver, is fed and armored well.

Of course, there is no "magic bullet" for weight loss and health – genetics, social relations, and activity level all play a huge part in why people live as long as they do and as well as they do. Some people can do everything right, never touch a cigarette or even be in the same room as a smoker and they die of lung cancer, other people might smoke like a chimney and live to be a comfortable 80. It's impossible to replicate in its entirety the life of a Sicilian peasant who ate tons of fat and lived to be 98, but you can reproduce some of the factors that are in your control, such as what you ate. At the end of the day, what we can control is ultimately infinitely more meaningful than the things we can't. It's important to keep this mind because there are so many things that are out of our power, but the first step to a healthier you is knowing that you, not anyone else, but YOU, are in complete control of how you fuel yourself.

What do I eat and how much?

The million-dollar question for any diligent dieter! Before you start chugging olive oil and eating whole fish, it's a good idea to get a firmer grasp on the food that comprises this diet, as I can repeat "olive oil, fish, wine, and wheat" all day but that could end in disaster from rancid oil, fast food fish, wine coolers, and saltine crackers.

As a first step, it's a good idea to avoid anything processed and any fast food if you're going to try to follow this diet. Not only are these not part of the plan, but these foods are addictive, fattening, and inflammatory, not to mention that their ingredients' list looks like something Frankenstein would cook up to get his monster lurching around and waxing dramatically. Much like how many healthy, whole foods are full of smaller health benefits than just what their known for – (did you know canned sardines are full of calcium, that's because you're eating BONES! Pressure cooked, soft bones, but bones nonetheless) processed foods and fast foods are the same way – the more you look the uglier they get.

Anyway, onto the meat of the issue. There isn't really a single, codified-by-the-USDA catch-all guide for following this diet, so these considerations are drawn from a handful of sources to form a comprehensive guide.

To be eaten every day at every meal are the staples; olive oil, bread, and other cereals like pasta or couscous, and vegetables. Eaten every day are beans, fruits, and nuts. Seafood should be eaten every day, red meat once a week, poultry every other day, eggs and dairy in moderate amounts, perhaps once to twice a day for dairy and once a day for eggs. Finally, red wine should be drunk in moderation, first of all, but every day.

For foods not on the list, such as vegetable oils, desserts, and sweets, use sparingly. There isn't necessarily anything wrong with "conventional" vegetable oil but its health benefits are smaller compared to olive oil. The one thing it beats olive oil in is high-heat cooking, but for that, I recommend deferring to the black sheep of the olive oil family, extra light olive oil. It can handle the higher smoke point but the flavor is lighter, so more suited for frying.

Coming to a new diet is never easy - the transition is always rocky and filled with self-doubt and regret, desire to turn back, but if your palate is adventurous and you subsist off things besides pizza and beer, you shouldn't have problems with the foods you're eating. The Mediterranean diet is very rich in variety, and home to some of the deepest and famous cooking cultures in the world, so if you like to cook or try new foods, you will be in good company. That is, provided you don't eat an entire basket of bread with every meal and take it as an excuse to knock back whole bottles of wine in one sitting.

A Quick Guide

It is to be said that in many countries of the Mediterranean, there is a much different food culture. I can't confidently speak for countries such as Morocco, Egypt, Turkey, and Tunisia, but in the countries that inspired the diet – Greece, Spain, and Italy, there is a big focus on enjoying life to its fullest with all its simple pleasures. The Italians have an expression "dulce far niente" – sweetness in doing nothing, the pleasant wasting of time.

These cultures are more traditional, and they take the time to appreciate as well as they can all of life's smaller pleasures, like food and family. Eating with people you love and care for, while obviously, it's not always a certainty, is as important as eating itself, it's what makes the food so significant. It's been shown time and time and again that strong social bonds are conducive to good health, from curbing anxiety and depression to more somatic, concrete benefits like easing hypertension and reducing general inflammation. This is not necessarily a part of the Mediterranean diet, but it is part of the lifestyle, and unfortunately, it is not feasible for all of us. But, if it's possible, try to fit the people that enrich your life in with the food that does the same, you'll find that it makes that glass of wine all the sweeter.

Chapter 2: How to Ensure Success

Far be it from me to presume, but chances are, you want your diet to work, whatever your goals may be. That's what the first half of this chapter is focused on – strategies to make sure that you get to where you want to go, strategies to keep you focused and your eye on the prize.

When it comes to goals, the most common is always wanting to shed weight, but there are always others – wanting to reduce the risk of heart problems or other chronic diseases, wanting to improve athletic performance in the weight room, the track, or otherwise. All these can be attained if you follow the diet with enough patience. Finally, a 28-day meal plan is included, free to twist and modify as little or as much as you want.

Number 1 way to ensure success: set a goal

When it comes to scaling any new summit, it's important to have a goal. The importance of planning cannot be understated, if multinational conglomerates and international superpowers do it, there must be something to it, and you always learn from those who are better than you. It's like a figurative path through a dark forest, something to guide you to make sure you don't trip on any obtrusive roots or wander into an errant witch's cabin, even if her house is made from cannolo shell. If you do it right, there are markers of progress along the way, and sticking to your diet is always easier when you can see the markers of success.

Usually, you have a pretty clear idea of why you're doing what you're doing. In the case of following the Mediterranean diet - maybe you're just interested in the diet, or maybe you have 3 months to lose 60 pounds before a machine rigged to your debit account drains your funds or some other cartoonish scheme goes into play. Whatever your reason, you need to turn your focus inward and start asking yourself some questions, like:

-Why am I doing this?

-What do I hope to gain from it?

-How do I get there?

Once these mountains are conquered, you can lay out the actual, serious groundwork and a real plan. It always helps to have things enunciated clearly, just the process of going through and saying "I want to do THIS because of THIS REASON, and I will do it LIKE THIS" is a powerful first step.

Generally, goal-setting, like everything else in life, is best taken one piece at a time. Break it into easy-to-swallow pieces, like those small, triangular, and delicious pieces of pita bread that you get from Mediterranean restaurants. Ask yourself those questions "Why am I doing this?" and the answer is "I need to lose weight," go on with "I hope that I can feel better, look better, and perform better, as well as be healthier." Finally, "I'll get there by following the Mediterranean diet and a regimented exercise program." Great, we've done some basic planning, more than a lot of people do, and ultimately, it will take you farther. Now that you've got your basic why, what, and how, you can figure the rest out, it's not as simple as winging and eating a box of pasta a day. Believe me, I've tried.

Once your goalposts are whittled down to the barest, simplest to understand nub, there's a bit of introspection that needs to be done. Go inside yourself and ask yourself where you are right now, you can't know where you're going until you know where you are at this moment. From there, it's easier to begin breaking down your goal into manageable pieces. A single goal like losing 60 pounds is a dragon, a beast - something that seems almost unmanageable. But if you're smart, and you break it down from where you are right now, then you have something to work with, a monster that you can slay.

So, your current weight is 200 pounds. You want to lose 60 pounds. How much do you want to lose each week? The amount of weight you aim to lose each week will become your micro-goal, your progress mile marker, so to speak, to make sure you're on track.

Keep in mind, each pound is about 3,500 calories, if we're talking fat, and we probably are, because most people don't want to lose muscle.

If your goal is 2 pounds of fat a week, that's roughly 1,000 less a day, every single week.

How would you get there? If you follow the Mediterranean diet, you can fill up on a lot of healthy olive oils, fibrous vegetables, fish, and bread for energy. The energy is something you'll need because the foundation of a healthy body and mind is exercise, which you'll have to combine with your new diet so you can lose your weight and properly armor your heart against the dangers of carrying excess weight.

Great, so, you've got a weekly plan. Try to cut down your calorie count by 1,000 a day and exercise. Weigh yourself every week to keep a measurement of how far you've gone every week.

The Importance of Recording

This brings us to the next important factor – keeping a record of some kind. Keeping a record is almost as important as the goal setting itself. It serves as physical evidence of your accomplishments. When you see it, you believe it, simple psychology does wonders for this sort of thing. It directly reinforces what you need to do. This may not come naturally or easily to many of you – that's okay, like many things of life, it's enforced via brutally beating it into your subconscious until it's a habit, and it's a habit that will serve you immeasurably throughout your life. Keep a journal of some kind, physical or otherwise, and keep a note that there are many smartphone and computer applications now that can track your calories for you, making it all the more easily to keep up.

Now that your goal is set and your "rate" so to speak, is established, you can estimate how long it will take you to reach this goal of yours.

You might be tempted to forgo the calorie-counting method altogether and just wing it, but I heavily advise against this. This is, first of all, hard to track. If you can't tell how much you ate one day and how much you ate the next, you're going to have no idea how many calories you ate for the week were. It's also a waste of time. Sure, it might work, you could wing it, see how much you could lose in a week by feeling it out, but it's not guaranteed to work. A month you spent winging it with bad results could have been a month you spent losing weight and moving closer to your goals.

A lesson in basic goal-setting may not be what you expected when you picked up this book, and it could come across as a bit presumptuous to any of you who are planners by nature or by profession, but the fact that it's in this book only serves to highlight why it's here. I couldn't give anyone a realistic and firm way to stick to their goal to get the results they want unless they knew how to plan, and while it seems basic, it's fundamental for any broad aspiration such as this.

Number 2: Pick Food You Like and Learn to Cook Them

An astounding revelation; this one should be sort of obvious, you'd think, right? Not necessarily! The numbers of people who are enamored with say carbs and a low carb diet and crash are innumerable. It's the same with anything, really – if you force yourself to do something you really hate for too long, there's no way you're going to succeed. As always, there are outliers, but that's all they are – outliers.

The Mediterranean diet is what I would call an "accepting" diet, it's flexible, and most of the time, people eat Mediterranean food without ever thinking about it. Pasta and pizza, while not always the healthiest choice, are some of the most ubiquitous foods in the world, and it seems like every grocery store in the world has about 40 different brands of olive oil.

There's no vegan or ketogenic dogma to follow, there's no low-fat low-salt no-fun foolishness to abide by, so that in and of itself automatically makes it easier for people. It's simple from there – identify holes you have in your diet, and then fill them with acceptable foods. If you need to get more fiber in your diet but you detest the taste and texture of whole-wheat pasta, don't cram it down. Have a serving of regular pasta to satiate your craving and cook up some vegetables with it, forgo it altogether and get your carbohydrate kick from whole wheat bread (and vegetables). If fish makes you want to puke, don't fret, as there are plenty of other protein options like eggs, poultry, yogurt and cheese, and red meat. If broccoli, kale, and cabbage aren't appetizing, don't just force it down because Cato the Elder said so, you'll just end up with your hand in a bag of chips again.

This is where it really pays off to know what's in the diet and know how to cook, it can really make dealing with unsavory or unpleasant foods easier if you know how to mask the taste with a fancy enough dish or even the right spices. To come back to fish, a food many people can't stand – if the "fishiness" or a certain species turns you off, it's easy to find plenty of mild-tasting fish (Whitefish like cod comes to mind, and has been part of the Mediterranean diet for hundreds of years in a dried, salted form) or forgo it entirely for something that has a similar nutritional profile. The closest thing in the Mediterranean diet to fatty wild fish would probably be ethically-raised dark meat chicken. Happy animals tend to have higher concentrations of omega-3s than ones kept in a slaughter dungeon and the dark meat is higher in fat.

Number 3: Cover Your Bases

A good diet is a balanced diet, and this may be the most crucial point for many people. If you're used to not eating carbs, one day, you might break and all of a sudden eat an entire loaf of bread in one sitting, which is metabolic hell for you and sends you spiraling. No, don't pursue any of that foolishness. Instead, make sure you get all your macronutrients – your fats, proteins, and carbohydrates – down. And make sure to drink enough water and eat enough fiber. Fat, protein, fiber, and water all play a huge part in making sure you feel full and keep cravings away, so getting enough of them is essential.

And while this is rare in the modern world, vegetables are necessary for avoiding vitamin and mineral deficiencies. Besides micronutrients, you need them for antioxidants and many other hard to spell and hard to remember compounds like phytopigments and other bioactive substances.

Number 4: Make Activity a Habit

Exercise is a necessary part of a healthy lifestyle and benefits everything from the brain to toes in ways too many to name.

The most obvious effect of exercise is mitigating eating an entire pizza – exercise is a must for keeping in shape and keeping your flab to a size not too embarrassing to show your compatriots in the locker room. Depending on the type of exercise you do, it can help your flexibility, strength, coordination, and balance. In addition, whenever you exercise, you're letting your brain open the endorphin channels, giving you what is biochemically a free opiate high. It can be psychologically satisfying too – pushing yourself through sessions is a lesson you can apply to all aspects of your life and you might even have a little fun along the way. Take some time to investigate and find your perfect fit when it comes to exercise. There's a school for almost every kind of person.

If committed time in the weight room, track, or otherwise isn't your thing, there are still simple strategies to get your calories down. A general recommendation handed out by doctors for exercise is 30 minutes a day – easy to do with a 10-minute walk after meals. If you have the option, take the stairs in your building, and if you work at a desk, consider moving to a standing desk. The more you put your brain in the game, the more daily ways of exercising appear.

Number 5: Practice Mindfulness

This can sound like a line of vague, new age mysticism, but bear with me. It's simply a matter of keeping in mind why you're following the diet. If it's weight loss, keep a strong, concrete idea of what you want out of it. It can be something simple, even if it's something that seems as vain as wanting to fit into a new outfit or impress your lover, anything is a valid reason if it helps you with your goal.

There is a philosophy that started in the Mediterranean in Greece and spread to Italy during the late Roman Republic. This philosophy is called Stoicism, founded by Zeno of Citium. It's not stoicism how it's typically thought about – a stone-faced man who never breaks his expression. One of its core tenants is that you are responsible for your happiness in every moment. You make the choice if you need that extra indulgence and you deal with the consequences; you and you alone. It emphasizes simple pleasures in life and not going into excess. Keep this idea in your mind when faced with temptation.

Next, take a hint from the people of the Mediterranean: enjoy your food. Eat slowly, deliberately, and savor every bite. You'll find that your gut has a slower reaction time than your brain, and when you practice this focused, almost meditative eating, the experience is more fulfilling and nourishing for the soul, and less for your fat cells. Do things like pause and have a thought between bites, put your fork down and chew. Whatever your ritual evolves to be, focus on slowing down.

Mentally gird yourself for what is to come. For many people, when changing diets and reflecting on their eating habits, their attitudes towards food change as well. Don't use it as an emotional crutch when you're sad or eat because you're bored. Those are bad habits and the lack of discipline can spread to all other parts of your life if you're not careful. Find another sponge for your emotions or way to use up your time – go hit the heavy bag, write down your feelings, go read a book, call a friend, anything to keep you from starting down a road laden with disaster. Don't eat your feelings!

And on the subject of feelings, try not to get discouraged when the inevitable happens. I'm not talking about death and taxes, but don't get discouraged by those either, I'm referring to the dreaded plateau. In anything in life, the beginning is always easier. The jumps are of huge magnitude and happen often, and as you progress, it gets harder. This is normal, and it's merely part of the game, something you have to ride out and get used to because there is no avoiding it, only weathering it. As long as you stick to your diet, things should iron out.

Number 6: Prepare Your Space

This is not some esoteric feng shui tactic of aligning your bottles of olive oil in the right geometric pattern to allow proper flow of chi. This is a two-fold approach to making sure that everything is in its right place; mind and space, for beginning your new diet.

To get a better grasp as to what I'm talking about, examine your kitchen. Anything that doesn't fit with the diet, make a note to not buy that again until your done with the diet. That way, there's no temptation of breaking into the box of cookies. Don't throw it away, give it away, or consciously choose that particular food when making meals, and when that's done, the other half of the plan comes into effect.

Set a date of when to officially start your diet. This fits in with making a plan. Optimally, this would be a part of your goal setting process. Once your date is set, you can go shopping and get only what you need for your diet. That way, as long as you're at home, it's essentially impossible to break.

Number 7: Eat Breakfast

No need to descend into a caloric underworld by having a full English breakfast, but have something, optimally with fiber, protein, and healthy fat, in the morning to get some fuel into the machine and the engine revving.

Those who eat early eat less – eight out of ten people who try to shear some fat off, and do it successfully, keep the habit. It's tempting to see why you might try to skip it, wake up, get some coffee down, and off you go until lunch, but breaking your fast early on shows that you will indulge less later on in the day, as it decreases appetite and wards away those gnawing impish feelings of hunger on the belly.

All the components of a good breakfast, complex carbohydrates, protein, and good fat, all of which are known to wield great power when it comes to the task of filling human bellies, are found easily with some searching. Demeter bears her bounty – whole wheat bread and vegetables are big parts of the Mediterranean diet, and if you can brave the strong flavor Poseidon has to offer, his children, the sardines, have both fat and protein. If you lack a palate strong enough for them, smoked salmon and eggs are both favorites that are nestled in comfortably with the rest of the diet.

How To Ensure Success For The Athletes

"No citizen has a right to be an amateur in the matter of physical training...what a disgrace it is for a man to grow old without ever seeing the beauty and strength of which his body is capable" – Socrates

Blessed are you who stand in the shadow of mighty Heracles, the athletes, and the Olympians. The Mediterranean countries in antiquity were known for their rigorous dedication to physical training, and this diet provided all they needed. To be the wrestler, weightlifter, team sports player, track, or boxer you were born to be, keep in mind a few considerations when following this diet.

The Mediterranean diet is very rich in carbohydrates, all the fuel you need to do your best on the field, but it might be best to keep them in their simple forms – bread and pasta – before your bouts, so the body can access them more easily, and complex – beans and whole wheat – after, to facilitate easier muscle growth. In addition, it's important to give your muscles as much as they need to rebuild themselves, so eat plenty of fish, yogurt, cheese, and poultry to keep yourself strong.

43

The 28-day Meal Plan

Before we get into the thick of it, there are a few things to ruminate on. First, this meal plan is not designed for everyone. It's more of a template – something that you can manipulate to your own devices as you need to, and the seven-day format means it can be repeated four times to be 28 total days.

When it comes to nutritional information, the daily calorie count from the American Dietary Guidelines was considered – that being a nice and even 2,000 kcal a day. The daily allotment of carbohydrates was taken to be 300 grams, or 60% of kcal, 56 grams of fat, about 25% of kcal, and finally around 75 grams of protein, the remaining 15% of your daily need. For fruits and vegetables, five servings of vegetables and two of fruit, and a total fiber need of 20-30 grams.

You will find that most of these recipes don't necessarily match up to the exact dietary guidelines; rather, they come in the ballpark of 2,000, usually with much higher protein content. The approach I used here was one more gauged toward attaining maximum fullness of the dieter as an approach for easy weight loss, which, of course, facilitates and enhances the other benefits of the Mediterranean diet; namely reduction of the chance of coronary heart disease and the encroaching diabetic threat upon the horizon – metabolic syndrome.

Many of the calorie counts are lower than the recommended amount; this is because when trying to lose weight, it's important that you keep the satiety up. How do you keep satiety up? By consuming more protein, fat, and fiber. In fact, when total calorie counts are lower and you're trying to lose weight, it's better to eat more protein. That reason is that the fewer carbs and fats you eat, the more protein you need to supplement to keep your body composition where it is. In addition, it can boost metabolism and increases the production of hormones that make you feel full. In addition, a phenomenon called the "thermal effect of food" – which is a scientific way of stating it takes more calories to consume protein (wrap your mind around that one). The effect is expressed as a percentage. In protein's case, this percentage is anywhere from 20-30%. This means, in a nutshell, that if you eat 100 calories of protein, you're really only eating 70-80. Carbohydrates and fat both have a much lower thermal effect, around 5-10% for carbs and only 0-3% for fat.

Finally, the last thing to note is that a lot of the protein comes from plant-based sources. Plant-based sources differ from animal sources in that they lack a few of the essential amino acids – the body needs nine, to produce the protein that your body can use to repair tissue, build muscle, all that good stuff. How do we get all the protein we're owed from plants? By supplementing with other plants; hence why the phenomena of rice and beans exist – the two eaten together yield all nine amino acids. That's why there's such a diversity of plant-based foods in this diet and in this plan because when eaten together, you get the protein you need.

As you're going through this, you're going to run across the term "net carbohydrates" a heck of a lot of times; and you may be telling yourself "I don't know what in Hades' decrepit realm a net carbohydrate is" but fear not, for the wisdom of Athena shines down upon you through my words. Carbs come in a few different forms such as sugar, starch, and fiber. Sugar can be broken down into component pieces, but that's not important for the purposes of this. Sugar and starch are used as energy, fiber is not. Net carbohydrate simply means the type of carbohydrate used for producing energy, essentially, the total carbohydrate content of the dish with the fiber subtracted.

You'll also notice I use the term "kilocalorie" versus "calorie." An actual calorie used in physics and in chemistry is one one-thousandth of a kilocalorie. A kilocalorie is merely a more exact count of the energy content in food – the calories you see on the nutrition facts are actually kcal.

Below are the references to keep in mind:

- kcal – kcal
- P - Protein
- F – Fat
- Fi –Fiber
- Net Carbs – Net Carbohydrates

- Carbohydrates - Carbs
- gr - grams

Day 1:

Breakfast: Fisherman's eggs (1 can of sardines, 3 eggs):

410 kcal, P: 41 gr, F: 26 gr

2 slices of whole wheat bread:

300 kcal, P: 14 gr, Net Carbs: 52 gr, F: 4 gr, Fi: 6 gr

Health benefits: Healthy protein and fat, omega-3s and calcium from the sardines.

Lunch: Mediterranean Wrap with cucumbers, tomato, onion, pita, spinach, lemon juice, hummus, feta cheese, and chicken breast (370 grams):

550 kcal, P: 34 gr, F: 22 gr, Net Carbs: 54 gr, Fi: 6 gr

Health benefits: The variety of vegetables include many micronutrients, protein, and fiber.

Dinner: 2 servings of grilled eggplant with olive oil (2 cups and .5 tablespoon of oil):

70 kcal, P: 2 gr, Net Carbs: 16 gr, F: 7 gr, Fi: 6 gr

1 cup cannellini beans:

255 kcal, P: 15 gr, Net Carbs: 47 gr, F: 1 gr, 11 Fi: gr

3 cups of Caesar salad:

480 kcal, P: 10 gr, Net Carbs: 23 gr, F: 40 gr, Fi: 6 gr

Health benefits: A ton of fiber from all three dishes and complex carbohydrates are helpful to keep your blood sugar and insulin stable. Protein comes from the beans and micronutrients come from the salad and eggplant.

Total: 2065 kcal, P: 116 gr, Net Carbs: 192 gr, F: 100 gr, Fi: 34 gr

Day 2:

Breakfast: Mediterranean Toast (5 Olives, 1 tomato, and a boiled egg on toasted ciabatta):

535 kcal, P: 16 gr, Net Carbs: 56 gr, F: 28 gr, Fi: 5 gr

1 Cup of 2% Greek yogurt:

165 kcal, P: 22 gr, Net Carbs: 9 gr, F: 4 gr

Health benefits: Bread is a good source of energy in the morning, monounsaturated fat from the olives, micronutrients and fiber from the tomato, and protein and fat from the egg. Greek yogurt is a source of probiotics, calcium, and a ton of protein.

Lunch: Greek Salad (Cucumber, tomato, feta cheese, red onion, a tablespoon of olive oil and red wine vinegar dressing) (160 grams):

180 kcal, P: 5 gr, Net Carbs: 8 gr, F: 10 gr and Fi: 2 gr

Roast chicken thigh:

140 kcal, P: 14 gr, F: 9 gr

Health benefits: Salad is high in fiber and micronutrients, healthy fats and protein from the cheese and oil. Dark meat chicken is a cheap and plentiful source of protein and is a richer source of minerals and vitamin B than white meat.

Dinner: 7oz Grilled salmon with oregano and dill:

410 kcal, P: 40 gr, F: 27 gr

Roast tomatoes, squash, and peppers with olive oil (1 of each vegetable, 1 tablespoon oil):

240 kcal, P: 5 gr, Net Carbs: 28 gr, F: 15 gr, Fi: 6 gr

Pasta and Tomato Sauce (250 grams):

270 kcal, P: 9 gr, Net Carbs: 49 gr, F: 5 gr, Fi: 5 gr

Health benefits: Salmon is a fantastic source of protein and good fats loaded with omega-3s. Roasted vegetables are full of vitamins, fiber, and minerals. Pasta and tomato sauce is great for energy and are a decent source of protein.

Total: 1940 kcal, P: 111 gr, Net Carbs: 150 gr, F: 98 gr, Fi: 18 gr

Day 3:

Breakfast: Eggs in Purgatory (3 eggs, .5 Cups sauce):

250 kcal, P: 20 gr, Net Carbs: 7 gr, F: 15 gr, Fi: 2 gr

Health benefits: Eggs are a good source of protein and fat, tomato sauce is a good source of lycopene.

Lunch: 2 cups Kale and tomato salad with 1 cup of roast chicken breast and tablespoon of pesto dressing:

365 kcal, P: 36 gr, Net Carbs: 20 gr, F: 18 gr, Fi: 5 gr

Slice of whole wheat bread:

150 kcal, P: 7 gr, Net Carbs: 26 gr, F: 2 gr, Fi: 3 gr

Health benefits: High in fiber, complex carbs, micronutrients, and protein

Dinner: 1 cup of Risotto:

415 kcal, P: 14 gr, Net Carbs: 54 gr, F: 13 gr, Fi: 2 gr

6oz Baked cod with lemon:

200 kcal, P: 41 gr, F: 2 gr

Boiled, stuffed artichokes:

480 kcal, P: 20 gr, Net Carbs: 60 gr, F: 21 gr, Fi: 11 gr

Health benefits: Cod is a lean protein source, artichokes are full of fiber, and risotto complements your energy needs that you're lacking from today's meal plan.

Total: 1850 kcal, P: 138 gr, Net Carbs: 167 gr, F: 71 gr, Fi: 23 gr

Day 4

Breakfast: 1 cup of 2% fat Greek yogurt:

165 kcal, P: 22 gr, Net Carbs: 9 gr, F: 4 gr

Whole wheat toast and butter:

270 kcal, P: 7 gr, Net Carbs: 26 gr, F: 16 gr, Fi: 3 gr

Health benefits: Fiber and good fat come from the bread. Greek yogurt is a good source of probiotics, protein, and calcium.

Lunch: 2 cups Arugula, walnut, and tomato salad with a tablespoon of red wine and olive oil dressing:

340 kcal, P: 9 gr, Net Carbs: 26 gr, F: 26 gr, Fi: 4 gr

6oz of smoked salmon

200 kcal, P: 32 gr, F: 8 gr

Cup of roast chickpeas:

255 kcal, P: 15 gr, Net Carbs: 47 gr, F: 1 gr, Fi: 11 gr

Health benefits: A ton of fiber and micronutrients comes from the salad. Chickpeas are fibrous and healthy protein sources. Smoked salmon is an awesome source of protein with omega-3s.

Dinner: Homemade mozzarella, artichoke heart, salami, mushroom, and spinach pizza (.38 of a 12-inch pie)

600 calories, P: 37 gr, Net Carbs: 113 gr, F: 20 gr, Fi: 7 gr

Health benefits: These are energy-rich and full of protein, fiber, and micronutrients.

Total: 1830 kcal, P: 122 gr, Carbs: 221 gr, Fi: 25 gr

Day 5

Breakfast: Tablespoon of Ricotta and fig spread on toasted Ciabatta bread:

340 kcal, P: 15 gr, Net Carbs: 59 gr, F: 9 gr, Fi: 4 gr

Two Boiled eggs:

140 kcal, P: 12 gr, F: 10 gr

Health benefits: Protein and fat come from the eggs while carbohydrates, protein, and healthy fat are from the toast.

Lunch: Whole Pita with 4 tablespoons of hummus:

265 kcal, P: 11 gr, Net Carbs: 33 gr, F: 13 gr, Fi: 14 gr

2 cups of steamed broccoli with half tablespoon olive oil and lemon:

270 kcal, P: 8 gr, Net Carbs: 42 gr, F: 9 gr, Fi: 5 gr

Health benefits: Pita and hummus combine to form a complete protein and are full of fiber and healthy fat, broccoli is similar; healthy fat from its olive oil and fiber and micronutrients.

Dinner: 1 cup of spinach, tomato, and caper orzo:

390 kcal, P: 15 gr, Net Carbs: 69 gr, F: 1 gr, Fi: 6 gr

8 ounces of Seared tuna:

300 kcal, P: 67 gr, F: 1 gr

2 cups roast asparagus with a tablespoon of olive oil:

200 calories, P: 9 gr, Net Carbs: 15 gr, F: 15 gr, Fi: 7 gr

Health benefits: Seared wild tuna is a great source of protein while the pasta and asparagus are rich sources of micronutrients and fiber.

Total: 1905 kcal, P: 137 gr, Net Carbs: 218 gr, F: 58 gr, Fi: 36 gr

Day 6

Breakfast: Flatbread (85g) with 1-ounce feta cheese tablespoon of olive oil and herbs:

430 kcal, P: 12 gr, Net Carbs: 48 gr, F: 21 gr, Fi: 2 gr

Cucumber and tomato salad with a tablespoon of olive oil and red wine vinegar

170 kcal, P: 2 gr, Net Carbs: 12 gr, F: 14 gr, Fi: 3 gr

Health benefits: Energy, protein, and healthy fat are from your bread and cheese. The salad has plenty of fiber and micronutrients.

Lunch:1 cup Calabrese salad

220 kcal, P: 13 gr, Net Carbs: 5 gr, F: 17 gr, Fi: 1 gr

Pasta with tomato sauce (250 grams)

270 kcal, P: 9 gr, Net Carbs: 49 gr, F: 5 gr, Fi: 5 gr

Health benefits: Energy and lycopene are from the pasta, while protein, fiber, and micronutrients are from the Calabrese salad.

Dinner: Rosemary roast pork loin (6oz)

325 kcal, P: 45 gr, F: 15 gr

Roast squash, tomato, and bell pepper in one tablespoon of tahini sauce.

210 kcal, P: 8 gr, Net Carbs: 31 gr, F: 9 gr, Fi: 9 gr

Cup of roast chickpeas:

255 kcal, P: 15 gr, Net Carbs: 47 gr, F: 1 gr, Fi: 11 gr

Health benefits: Excellent source of protein in the pork, micronutrients and fiber in the vegetables, and protein, energy, and fiber in the chickpeas.

Total: 1880 kcal, P: 106 gr, Net Carbs: 192 gr, F: 79 gr, Fi: 30 gr

Day 7

Breakfast: 3 fried eggs fried in half tablespoon olive oil

330 kcal, P: 18 gr, F: 29 gr

10 olives

45 kcal, Net Carbs: 2 gr, F: 4 gr, Fi: 1 gr

6 dried dates

120 kcal, P: 1 gr, Net Carbs: 32 gr, Fi: 3 gr

Health benefits: Protein and fat from the eggs, monounsaturated fat from the olives, carbs, micronutrients, and fiber from the dates.

Lunch: 2 cups Tortellini in broth

210 kcal, P: 11 gr, Net Carbs: 33 gr, F: 5 gr, and Fi: 3 gr

2 cups of Greek salad (Cucumber, tomato, feta cheese, red onion, tablespoon of olive oil and red wine vinegar dressing)

360 kcal, P: 10 gr, Net Carbs: 15 gr, F: 30 gr, Fi: 4 gr

Health benefits: Fiber and micronutrients are from the salad while the soup is a good source of electrolytes, carbohydrates, and protein.

Dinner: 6 oz New York strip:

530 calories, P: 44 gr, F: 37 gr

2 cup steamed broccoli, carrots, and cauliflower with tablespoon lemon and olive oil

210 kcal, P: 4 gr, Net Carbs: 14 gr, F: 15 gr, Fi: 6 gr

2 cups of garlic couscous:

350 kcal, P: 12 gr, Net Carbs: 72 gr, Fi: 4 gr

Health benefits: Couscous is a good source of energy and fiber, broccoli is great for its micronutrient profile and fiber, and steak is full of proteins.

Total: 2,155 calories, P: 94 gr, Net Carbs: 168 gr, F: 120 gr, Fi: 21 gr

Chapter 3: Shopping Guide

So, you've decided to take a perilous plunge into the unknown and try out a new diet. Great. Where do you begin? Probably by eating the food, if I had to guess. What if you don't have the food? Well, that's what this guide is for, it's a complete shopping guide for those of us looking to follow the Mediterranean diet; with a special section on how to eat on a budget. So, if you're looking to start, and have absolutely no idea what specific sorts of food to buy (I can say "wheat, fish, olives, and wine all day), this is your saving grace.

For eating on a budget:

Let this be squared away now. Most diets are feasible on a budget, it just takes some creativity, skill, craftiness, and if you're really destitute, the willingness to eat possibly strange foods. The diet of the Mediterranean is a diet of the poor – it was based on the eating habits of poor rural farmers. Some of the foods listed are expensive and there is nothing to be done about that – good olive oil comes to mind, but many other factors can be mitigated with the right touch, palate, and knowing where to look.

It was said in the last chapter, and it's being said again here to reinforce how important this one particular skill is for making your diet, and, to a lesser extent, for your life to perform better for you. That skill is learning to cook. For those of us who are lacking in funds, this is a great way to plug any holes in your diet. Unless you're constantly buying the most expensive base products you can get, this is a sure way of stretching every sestercius (sestertius was a form of currency in ancient Rome). When I say base – I mean the basest thing you can get, nothing prepared, no pre-rolled tortellini, no microwave meals, or no frozen breaded chicken. If it looks easy to prepare and eat, ignore it, because you can't afford it. Or at least act like you can't. And when I say base, I mean base. Plain dried pasta, whole chickens, that sort of thing. Your spice rack is a powerful friend and ally – use it well, learn what you like with what kind of foods. If you're brave enough to try making bread (It's really not hard) pick up flour and yeast. If the people of the ancient (and modern) Mediterranean could do it, so can you. Consider starting your own garden so you aren't blowing money on herbs and vegetables every week as well. This will be covered in the final chapter. It's also a way to control your nutrient content, portion out meals to be eaten later, and it's a fun and impressive skill.

More considerations:

- When you're buying something you know you're going to be using a lot of (Olive oil, flour, etc.) that stays good for a long time, buy in bulk. Buying in bulk is always cheaper per whatever unit we're counting, and if you can properly preserve your goods, all the more power to you. As long as your oil is properly capped, and your flour is sealed away, it should be able to nourish you for months to years. Years more for the case with flour – oil eventually goes rancid.

- Think about where you get your goods. Even if you're buying off-brand products, depending on the store, they can be more expensive. Consider shopping at places like big box stores or known savings/discount stores. If they're available in your area, check out a farmer's market, as haggling is usually an option there, and if what you're looking for is in season, it'll be cheaper. Ethnic stores are also an option, as many of them sell cheaper meat and eggs than many bigger chains.

- When you look for animal protein, there are some tenants to consider. Cold cuts are almost always far, far more expensive per pound, so unless you catch a deal, you can pretty much overlook those. Beef is far more expensive than both pork and poultry, and tough cuts of beef or pork are always going to be cheaper than the better, more aristocratic cuts. Learning some basic butchery would be a help, too – chicken is cheaper than both but can be cheaper if you buy a whole chicken and learn to split it yourself. It's not a skill that takes forever to learn, and it makes portioning out your meals easier. If you can't get the hang of things, some of the cheapest chicken per pound is always leg quarters, and separating drumstick from thigh is a simple cut of the knife. Save the bones, too – useful if you're either a witch or just looking to make some tasty soup.

- Eating the huge amount of produce Mediterranean people eat can get expensive quick. If you find yourself broke trying to eat five servings of vegetables a day, buy your produce frozen. It keeps longer and none of the nutrients are lost when they're frozen. Avoid canned vegetables like the plague. They're oftentimes so pressure-cooked; they're essentially just flavored fiber.

- Learn how to meal-prep. Meal prep can turn a $15 grocery run into food for a week if you do it right. Try to make huge batches of cheap, healthy food. Chicken stock with beans and leftover meat can be frozen, reheated with fresh vegetables dropped in for a healthy, filling meal.

- Eat organ meat. A little spooky at first, and maybe a little hard to get used to, taste and texture wise, but undoubtedly the cheapest meat around. When the Pinarii and Potitii families of ancient Rome performed their yearly bull sacrifice to Heracles, they would eat all the meat, even the organs. Be like these families, be like Heracles. Offal – the culinary term, is nutritious and has a lot of unique flavors as opposed to "normal" meat. Besides the protein, you'll be getting a significant dose of micronutrients for your money.

- If you're already snooping around a farmer's market for fresh produce, you may as well ask the farmers if they have any organ meat they're willing to part with.

- When it comes to cooking this mysterious organ meat – take it slow, take it steady. Don't try a pig head soup with stewed chicken feet and blood broth. That's a surefire way to make sure you never eat anything of that sort again. You've got to ease your way in – there are many ways to kill the taste of one particularly nutritious piece of offal – liver, which has the unfortunate property of tasting sort of like dog food. That is to soak the liver in milk for the entire evening. Other foods like heart and tongue are pretty much identical, tissue-wise, to regular muscle meat. The tongue has a second home in a beef stew and beef heart can be stewed as well, or even just seared and sliced thin like a good steak. If none of this is working, try mixing it with ground meats and seasoning to make an offal meatball or meatloaf. All the benefits with watered-down flavors.

- Dairy products and eggs are your friends, really. The Mediterranean diet isn't excessively high in these foods, but if you can't afford meat, eat your fill of these two foods. They essentially provide all the same nutrition of meat, with a much smaller price tag. Yogurt is incredibly healthy besides the protein and fat content, as it has probiotics. Eggs are sometimes called the perfect food, because of their macronutrient content, and, if from happy chickens, contain high amounts of omega-3s.

- Seafood is usually expensive. Picking good seafood can be difficult, and it may warrant picking up fishing as a hobby, which is a subject for a different book. When picking a farmed seafood, always look at the country of origin, as many countries have more-or-less lax laws regarding aquaculture. Farmed seafood from a good, not too sketchy country can be nearly as nutritious as wild, and in some cases, more. If you can stomach it, canned wild fish and other seafood is much cheaper than fresh or even frozen versions and loses none of its nutritional value. As a side benefit, it also essentially has no expiration date.

- Another "get through life that much easier tip" is to remember to hunt for sales. Most grocery stores offer weekly sales on basic foodstuffs which contain carbohydrates, proteins, fats, and vegetables, and these sales will be your friend.

- Lastly, avoid anything pre-made. This includes eating out when you can help it. Obviously, we can always avoid social pressures, but if you can pass, pass. Frozen foods, deli foods, and things of that sort are always more expensive than just throwing something together.

Now that that's established, let us proceed into the rest of the shopping guide! To fit with this theme earlier in the chapter, foods will be broken up into "budget," "doing okay," and "comfortable amount of disposable income" brackets, though some will not need this sort of categorization.

Fats

Extra virgin olive oil (120 kcal per tablespoon, Fats: 14 gr, 10 grams monounsaturated, 2 polyunsaturated and 2 saturated) – Who knew this would be here? The world never ceases to surprise. Extra virgin olive oil is the most important part of the diet and boasts a variety of health benefits. It is good for the skin, hair, the heart, and may be able to control diabetes, and is tasty to boot. When it comes to buying the foundation of the diet, this is where it's permissible to spend a little cash. Good extra virgin olive oil is worth its weight in gold; because it's somewhat hard to come by.

"Wait a minute!" You say, my grocery has 57 varieties of it! That's where I say to take a seat – many commercial brand olive oils from Europe and North Africa are diluted with cheaper oils, so you aren't getting the real stuff at all. Interestingly, the United States, despite not being a Mediterranean country, has much higher standards for extra virgin olive oil, so always buy this kind of oil from the United States. California, with its Mediterranean climate, produces some of the best in the world.

Extra-light olive oils (120 kcal per tablespoon F: 14 grams, 10 grams monounsaturated, 2 polyunsaturated, and 2 saturated) – While there is a whole spectrum of olive oils to use, extra light and extra virgin are the best ones to go for. Both have certain cardiovascular-supporting effects, the high amount of unsaturated fats, namely, with the extra virgin having a stronger taste and more micronutrients, but extra-light olive oil has a unique culinary purpose. Extra-light olive oil is the best oil in the Mediterranean diet for high-heat frying and grilling, it has a lighter flavor and can stand up to smoke points its extra virgin compatriots can't. As for where to get it, extra light olive oil is far cheaper and easier to produce, and therefore, usually when you buy it from overseas, it actually is what it says it is, so the cheaper and bigger the bottle, the better.

Carbohydrates

Bargain:

Flour (30 kcal, P: 1 gr, Net Carbs: 6 gr – Unbleached and the biggest container you can find. Flour has a whole number of uses – making bread and pasta, thickening soups and stews, breading meat, it's just a convenient thing to have around your kitchen, and you'll never know when you might need it.

Wheat flour (25 kcal a tablespoon, P: 1 gr, Net Carbs: 5 gr, Fi: 1 gr) – The same as above, wheat flour is exactly the same as regular white flour, but with the hull of the wheat left on, so it has more fiber and micronutrients. It is great for making healthy, whole wheat bread and biscuits.

(Author's note: these two are filed under "bargain," because they're the cheapest thing available when it comes to carbohydrates and also because they are the building block of many commercially available foods, but they're good to always have around in your kitchen, no matter how much money you have.)

Dry beans (350 kcal, P: 21 gr, Net Carbs: 63 gr, F: 1 per 100 grams) – Cheap, nutritious, tasty and filling, and the basis of many Mediterranean dishes. It is a good source of protein when paired with pasta, bread, or rice. It can be used in soups, stews, eaten by themselves, or with a side of rice. Look for store brands. The most popular beans eaten in the Mediterranean are great northern beans, chickpeas, navy beans, fava beans, and cannellini beans.

Long-grain rice (200 kcal, P: 4 gr, Carbs: 45 gr, Fi: 1 gr per 1 cup uncooked) – Long grain rice is cheap, abundant, and versatile. Pair it with beans to make a complete protein, and always buy store brand in bulk.

Potatoes (160 kcal, P: 4 gr, Net Carbs: 37 gr, Fi: 5 gr) – This is a very cheap, very tasty, and very nutritious vegetable that resembles a rock. Usually, they come in bulk bags at grocery stores, and their sweet variety has even more nutrition than the conventional. Keep the skin on, that's where most of the fiber and micronutrients are.

Doing okay:

Pre-made whole wheat bread (150 kcal, P: 7 gr, Net Carbs: 26 gr, F: 2 gr, Fi: 3 gr – depends on serving size) – Whole wheat bread is a good source of complex carbohydrates and fiber. A word of warning when purchasing though, make sure that the first ingredient actually is whole wheat, or you could be getting shafted in the fiber department. Most grocery stores have store brand whole wheat and cheaper brands available, and some even have bakeries where you can get it made in-store.

White bread in all forms (100 kcal, P: 3 gr, Carbs: 18 gr, F: 1 gr, Fi: 1 gr per slice, size varies) – White bread in all forms is an energy-rich component of the Mediterranean diet, and has a variety of uses, both simple and complex. This includes all forms of bread like ciabatta, Portuguese rolls, flatbreads, pita, French, or Cuban bread. Make sure not to eat too much of this, though, as white bread can make you crash, fast from the blood sugar increase, and if you eat too much without exercising, can lead to weight gain.

Pasta (200 kcal a serving, P: 7 gr, Carbs: 38 gr, F: 1 gr) - Pasta has gotten a bad rap, but it can be part of a healthy diet if used correctly. It's energy-rich, filling, and very versatile. It often goes on sale, and store brands are indistinguishable from name brands for most people. Try it with a little bit of oil, garlic, and chili pepper. Simple, quick and tasty.

Short-grain rice (200 kcal, P: 4 gr, Carbs:45 gr, Fi: 1 gr per 1 cup uncooked) - The more expensive cousin of long-grain, used for things like risotto and other Mediterranean rice dishes. To mitigate the higher cost, always buy more and buy the store brand, unless you have a very distinguished rice-eating palate.

Comfortable amount of disposable income:

Sprouted grain bread (80 kcal, P: 4 gr, Net Carbs: 15 gr, F: 1 gr, Fi: 3 gr per slice) – Bread made from grain that has been milled after it's sprouted – healthier in many ways, higher in fiber, smaller insulin impact, but fairly expensive.

Wild rice (570 kcal, P: 24 gr, Net Carbs: 120 gr, F: 2 gr, Fi: 10 gr per 1 cup uncooked) – This is full of nutrients and also a high cost. It is not really rice at all, more like a strain of wild grasses. Good if you can afford it, but not a necessity.

Quinoa (120 kcal, P: 4 gr, Net Carbs: 21 gr, F: 2 gr, Fi: 3 gr) – This is trendy crop originating in South America, where it was once the staple crop of the native people. As it has immensely grown in popularity, its price has gone up. It has a high nutrient profile and is one of the few sources of complete plant protein (all nine amino-acids).

Couscous (175 kilocalories, P: 6 gr, Net Carbs: 36 gr, Fi: 2 gr) –
Good for energy and a decent source of fiber and potassium, but
despite its high price tag, there is nothing that's remarkable
about it, health-wise. Nothing particularly bad, but if you're
hurting for cash and need to make sure your body is where it
needs to be, there are better choices.

Meat and Seafood

Bargain:

Organ meat (Depends on the cut) – These are the heart, liver,
stomach lining, and those other wonderful bits of an animal.
They boast unique tastes, textures, and health benefits, for a low
price, but definitely, do not match everyone's palate. There are a
plenty variety of it, though, so if one isn't your fancy, there's a
completely different version to try.

Eggs (70 kcal, P: 6 gr, F: 5 per egg) – The easiest cheap protein to
get down if you're lacking in funds. They are very versatile and
very affordable, and has a home in Mediterranean dishes like the
frittata and the Spanish tortilla, and usually just a few dollars for
a dozen, and cheaper if you buy in bulk. Eggs raised by local
farmers with more humane practices are usually higher in
micronutrients such as omega-3s.

Chicken quarters in bulk (475 kcal, P: 62 gr, F: 23 gr per quarter) – The leg of the chicken. It's important to note that this is in bulk. Many grocery stores sell chicken quarters for less than the component piece, thigh or drumstick, when bought still attached to each other. They're easy to separate, have higher amounts of micronutrients, and work better for many chicken dishes than the more expensive breast does.

Bones (Depends how you make them) – This is a recommendation for the bargain section, but everyone should consider them. Making broth from bones is easy and nutritious, with collagen and protein. They can serve as the basis for soups, stews, beans, you name it, and can be frozen to last indefinitely.

Doing okay:

Farmed seafood (Depends on the product) – Fish is a major part of the Mediterranean diet, and as long as they're sourced from ethical farms, they're almost as good as the wild varieties. They come in all shapes and sizes, tilapia, salmon, swordfish, shrimp, crabs, and more varieties I can't possibly think of, and they're all healthy sources of protein. If you're buying salmon, it has a ton of omega-3s as well.

Canned seafood (Depends on the product) – Usually, canned seafood is wild, which is a good thing. Oftentimes, they're packed with bones, which is great, as pressure-cooked bones are easy to chew and a healthy source of calcium. They also last essentially forever, are versatile, and a good source of omega-3s and excellent quality protein. In addition, because most of them are tiny and thus the losers of the fish world and low on the food chain, their mercury count is significantly lower than the larger varieties. Small fish are a staple amongst people of the Mediterranean - sardines with pasta is a classic Sicilian dish and their health effects have been lauded for thousands of years.

Plebian cuts of meat AKA roasts (Depends on the cut) – Despite having a reputation of being "cheap," the price of these tough cuts have shot up in recent years. Think things like pork shoulder, picnic hams, beef chuck roast, round roast, and flank and brisket. Usually, they're full of collagen from connective tissue, which needs to be broken down via wet cooking, braising. The collagen is great for skin, hair, and nails, a side benefit beside the complete sources of protein. They take some skill to get right, but with a competent cook, they can be richer than the most expensive pieces of meat.

Chicken breast (366 kcal, P: 55 gr, F: 14 gr) – White meat chicken. Good for a clean source of protein, but somewhat expensive for what you're getting. Also, fairly easy to dry out or make rubbery with the wrong cooking techniques; this is not at all a pleasant to eat.

Whole chicken (Depends on the piece) – These used to be cheaper per pound, but as the years have gone on, at most stores they've climbed up the socioeconomic ladder of meat. On the upside, you're getting a lot of value. There's a lot of meat on that carcass, and buying them in one piece is always cheaper than buying the whole thing broken down. There's a skill to be learned here, as well, in the art of butchery. You can break it down into its component pieces and freeze what you don't use, or cook the whole thing at once and use the skeleton for stock.

Ground meats and sausage (Depends on the fat percentage) – Usually comes in turkey, beef, chicken, and pork. Beef tends to be the most expensive, pork the least, but if their fat content is the same, they should be pretty much identical in regards to cooking. They fit well with a lot of dishes - meatballs, meat sauce, and meatloaf, and go on sale often.

Cold cuts (100 kcal per slice, Net carbs: 41 gr, F: 9 gr) – Cold cuts have a long history in the Mediterranean. As most of its population throughout history, in rural Italy and Spain, especially, were poor, they needed to find a way to supplement their protein intake somehow. That's where cured and smoked meats - salume, bacon, smoked fish, serrano ham, prosciutto, and the like come in. Expensive, but nothing absurd unless you're buying European imports. A word of warning, though, as they are processed. Processed meat has been linked to a higher incidence of GI cancer than standard meat from the elements used to make sure they don't decay, so enjoy in moderation.

Comfortable amount of disposable income

Wild seafood (Depends on the product) – The king of healthy proteins to many people. Purchased fresh, are absolutely delicious, and full of omega-3s and vitamin D. Tuna, salmon, cod, swordfish, squid, and shrimp are all staples of the Mediterranean diet even today. Seafood roe and caviar also falls into this category.

Patrician cuts of meat (Depends on the product) – Your steaks, your pork loins and tenderloins, your prime quality, grass-fed, and all that. All these products boast a fair number of health benefits, they're usually lower in fat than other cuts, and if they're raised the right way they have a higher content of omega-3s and other healthy compounds, but you pay for it in the price tag. Side benefit: They're tasty, but don't screw it up. A waste of meat is a tragedy.

Vegetables

Vegetables are rarely expensive food; but with this in mind, it's important to eat a lot of them. Keeping your diet bright is a great way to make sure that you're getting almost everything you need in it.

Bargain:

Frozen vegetables (depends on vegetables) – Frozen vegetables have all the same benefits as their warmer friends, and they're far cheaper and usually sold in sacks similar in size to Santa Claus' sack of toys, which is a huge amount. The main downside as far as I can see is that when you freeze them, they usually come out tasting a little bit worse and their texture is almost rubbery, in a way.

Green cabbage (20 kcal, P: 1 gr, Net Carbs: 4 gr, Fi: 2 gr per cup) – Consistently the cheapest vegetable I've seen in the grocery store, as well as a major obsession of early Mediterranean writers, who were convinced it would solve the "Germanic problem" (that part not verified by any Classics department anywhere). It's full of micronutrients – vitamins and minerals, helps relax inflammation, and it can go in a wide variety of different foods. Try boiling cabbage in some bone broth with beans – simple and comforting.

Doing okay:

Other cruciferous vegetables (depends on type) – Kale, broccoli, cauliflower, cabbage of all colors of the rainbow, bok chow, Brussel sprouts, all these guys are what you want to be eating a lot of. When it comes to vegetables with a strong nutritional punch, you'll struggle to find any group as strong as these guys. Fiber, antioxidants, micronutrients like vitamin K and A, and plant phytonutrients and pigments all make these an essential part of the diet.

Peppers, all (30 kcal, P: 2 gr, Net Carbs: 7 gr, Fi: 1 gr) – The hot and the sweet peppers are very common around the Mediterranean sea, as it's one of the best climates for them. Full of vitamin C, they're a great addition to salads, with chicken or eggs, or to eat with dry meat. Spicy peppers are eaten in hotter parts of the Mediterranean because the sweating they make you do help you cool off.

Tomatoes (20 kcal, P: 1 gr, Net Carbs: 5 gr, Fi: 2 gr) – Great on salads, roasted, in sandwiches or by themselves, tomatoes boast a high vitamin A, C, and lycopene content. If you want to make a sauce, look no further than their canned varieties – picked at their freshest and ready-to-be-used to make a rich pasta or pizza sauce.

Asparagus (20 kcal, P: 2 gr, Net Carbs: 3 gr, Fi: 2 gr per 5 spears) – If I was trying to create a Macedonian phalanx sculpture out of food, I would use this for their spears. I don't know how that's relevant, but it's related to the Mediterranean. Asparagus is easy to cook up either in the oven, grill, or pan, and full of antioxidants and fiber.

Squashes (depends on breed) – Great for roasting and usually relatively inexpensive. Like all vegetables, fibrous and full of micronutrients like vitamin A and C. If you're feeling experimental, try replacing noodles with a variety made from squash like zucchini or summer squash.

Cucumber (30 kcal, P: 1 gr, Net Carbs: 7 gr, Fi: 1 gr per cucumber) – The closest thing on earth to being able to eat a glass of water. Refreshing and nourishing, cucumbers are great in salads and have high amounts of micronutrients and antioxidants in the skin and seeds.

Spinach (40 kcal, P: 5 gr, Net Carbs: 7 gr, F: 1 gr, and Fi: 4 gr per cup) – No longer solely for nautical strongmen who need to uppercut bullies into the moon, spinach is a powerful source of vitamins A, calcium, and a vegetarian iron source, although less bioavailable than animal iron, so eat it with some lemon juice to absorb more.

Eggplant (35 kcal, P: 1 gr, Net Carbs: 9 gr, Fi: 3 gr per cup) – A famous flavor sponge. It is great sautéed in olive oil with tomatoes but remember to salt it and let it sit first.

Mushrooms (45 kcal, P: 3 gr, Net Carbs: 8 gr, F: 1 gr, Fi: 3 gr per cup) – Not just for stuffing anymore. Mushrooms are great for their meaty texture, fiber, and high antioxidant count, great for a vegetarian replacement for meat and making your foods just a little more hearty.

Comfortable amount of disposable income:

Heirloom vegetables (Depends on variety) Heirloom tomatoes, Romanesco broccoli, purple carrots, and other rare and forgotten vegetable varieties are placed here. Chances are they don't differ much, nutritionally, from other vegetables, but their unique colors, textures, and flavors give them a greater price tag.

Fruit

To attempt to cover all the fruits available in this diet would be folly; instead, we've covered some of the more common examples.

Bargain

Grapes (30 kcal, Net Carbs: 9 gr per 10 grapes) – This is the classic Mediterranean choice. It has a decent amount of vitamin C and manganese.

Apples (95 kcal, P: 1 gr, Net Carbs: 25 gr, Fi: 4 gr per apple) – This is the fruit that Paris gave to the fairest at the beginning of the Iliad. It has fiber and phytonutrients that can help against cancer, heart disease, and diabetes.

Citrus of all varieties (depends on fruit) – The Mediterranean is an easy climate for citrus to grow in, and many countries feature these bright foods as part of their cuisine. Lemon, in particular, is a star, as it a very common flavoring ingredient in many Mediterranean foods.

Doing okay:

Fig (35 kcal, Net Carbs: 10 gr, Fi: 2 gr per fig) – Enjoyed since antiquity, the fig is a great accompaniment to dishes and by itself as a snack, dried or fresh. Enjoy in moderation.

Dates (20 kcal, Net Carbs: 5 gr, Fi: 1 gr per date) – Famous for being simultaneously the closest thing to candy found in nature, dates are an indulgence good for a quick energy boost, but be careful not to go too crazy with them because of the high sugar content.

Pineapple (40 kcal, P: 1 gr, Net Carbs: 11 gr, Fi: 1 gr per half cup) – A fruit known for eating you back because of its high bromelain content, when consumed in appropriate quantities, it can help fight inflammation.

Pomegranate (120 kcal per serving, P: 2 gr, Net Carbs: 27 gr, F: 2 gr, Fi: 6 gr per half fruit) – This is the fruit Hades enticed Persephone with and has a long history in the Mediterranean. A degree of fiber and polyphenols make this another star.

Avocado (230 kcal, P: 3 gr, Net Carbs: 12 gr, F: 21 gr, Fi: 9 gr) – A nutritional darling, avocados have an extremely high nutrient profile and are known for being a uniquely "buttery" fruit – having a very high monounsaturated fat content from their rich flesh.

Olive (5 kcal, F: .5 gr per olive) – Who could imagine olives being in this diet? The world gets crazier by the day, let me tell you. Olives come in a bunch of different varieties, green, black, purple, (I'm not kidding, they're marinated in red wine.) and stuffed, along with different curing techniques for different flavors. The thing to remember is they're all good sources of monounsaturated fat.

Comfortable amount of disposable income:

To save space, know that most fruits tend to fall in a moderate price range, the only time they get really expensive is out of season or if you're buying all organic fruit.

Dairy

Bargain:

Plain yogurt (110 kcal, P: 9 gr, Net Carbs: 12 gr, F: 3 gr for six ounces) – Plain yogurt is here because of its versatility and its probiotics. Buying Greek yogurt pre-made can ramp up costs, but with some cheesecloth and a lot of patience, you can do it at home. Plus, you can save the leftover whey for baked goods.

Making your own yogurt also deserves a spot. With the bacteria in a yogurt sample and treating your milk the right way with exactly the right heat, making yogurt at home is easy and time-consuming but very cheap per calorie.

Block cheese (110 kcal, P: 6 gr, Net Carbs: 1 gr, F: 9 gr per one ounce slice) – Notice I said block cheese, the kind you buy in a large, whole chunk, not processed "American" cheese. Think the giant blocks of Kraft provolone or cheddar. Cheese can be an incredibly rich source of nutrients, but buying imported, hard, aged cheeses can be expensive. While nowhere near the quality of a good pecorino or feta cheese, the block cheese still nourishes you with protein, calcium, vitamin D, and fat.

Cheese sticks (85 kcal, P: 6 gr, Net Carbs: 1 gr, F: 6 gr per stick) – Roughly Not made from the best quality cheese, but nothing really wrong with it, cheese sticks are convenient snacks that are roughly the equivalent of an egg per stick.

Doing okay:

Greek yogurt (135 kcal, P: 23 gr, Net Carbs: 8 gr, F: 1 gr for 8 ounces of 2%) – Strained yogurt with its liquid component removed. Recently gained fame in the health community for its high protein content and probiotic nature, if you can get used to the acidic taste. If you have a hard time getting used to it, try upping the fat content of the yogurt, generally the higher the fat, the easier it is to get down.

Hard cheese (110 kcal, P: 6 gr, Net carbs: 1 gr, F: 9 gr per one ounce piece) – These are your hard, grating cheeses, your parmiggiano, manchego, that sort of thing. They can be expensive per pound, but usually, are sold in modest enough sizes and are used sparingly enough to last a long time.

Kefir (110 kcal, P: 11 gr, Net Carbs: 12 gr, F: 2 gr per cup) – Coming from a Caucasian word meaning "to feel good," kefir is an admittedly weird, fizzy dairy drink that is very high in probiotics. Good for restoring the fauna of your gut after a night of guzzling red wine.

Comfortable amount of disposable income:

Skyr (185 kcal, P: 18 gr, Net Carbs: 27 gr, Fi: 1 gr per 8 ounce-serving) – Skyr is the fancy Icelandic version of yogurt, known for its milder taste and consistency. It's somewhat expensive compared to other forms of yogurt, and hard to make at home, thus listed here as something of a delicacy.

Nuts, seeds, legumes, and their ilk

Bargain:

Peanuts (165 kcal, P: 7 gr, Net Carbs: 6 gr, F: 14 gr, Fi: 2 gr per ounce) - The cheapest and most underrated nut. It goes great with stir-fries, grilled meat, or as a snack by itself. It has high amounts of minerals like copper and manganese.

Doing okay:

Almonds (170 kcal, P: 6 gr, Net Carbs: 6 gr, F: 15 gr, Fi: 3 gr per ounce) - Their flavors are featured heavily in Mediterranean desserts; almonds can be used like peanuts in many dishes. They are also a good source of biotin and vitamin E.

Walnuts (185 kcal, P: 4 gr, Net Carbs: 4 gr, F: 18 gr, and Fi: 2 gr per ounce) - When consumed with the skin on, it can be very nutritional. It has flavonoids and other antioxidants in abundance, with copper and omega-3s found in its flesh.

Sesame (160 kcal, P: 5 gr, Net Carbs: 7 gr, F: 14 gr, Fi: 4 gr per ounce) – It is a popular flavoring component in the Middle East, both by itself and in tahini. It is a good source of omega-3s, copper, and manganese.

Comfortable amount of disposable income:

Pistachio (160 kcal, P: 6 gr, Net Carbs: 8 gr, F: 13 gr, Fi: 3 gr per ounce) - Like all nuts, they are high in monounsaturated fat, rich in potassium, and vitamin B6.

Macadamia (200 kcal, P: 2 gr, Net Carbs: 4 gr, F: 21 gr, and Fi: 2 gr) – Not just in cookies anymore! Macadamia nuts are incredibly rich and are great sources of monounsaturated fat, iron, magnesium, potassium, and zinc, and a bunch of other nutrients I can't fit into this short description. If you can afford them, they're great for you.

Drinks

For the sake of simplicity, this will be kept in one section. It goes without saying that the main thing you should be drinking is water; water keeps you hydrated and brings sensations of fullness. You're 72% water, so it makes sense. Doctors recommend somewhere between 6-10 glasses a day, what no one tells you is that a lot of your hydration you get from food, so no need to just chug two-liter bottles like a neurotic mess.

Unsweet tea and coffee are also appropriate, Italians are known to enjoy tea with a hint of lemon, so see if that tickles your fancy. Coffee, in many parts of the Mediterranean, is drunk in espresso form, easily made with a stovetop coffee pot, no need to dump $3,000 into an espresso maker. There are certain blends sold pre-ground designed for the machines, so keep an eye out for that.

And the drunken elephant in the room; red wine. Red wine comes with a dizzying amount of variety. There really is nowhere for me to start recommending wines, I'd simply suggest you avoid the swill. Don't buy any Mad Dog 2020, pink Moscato, or wine coolers and spend around $8 to $10 a bottle, as there's some real magic out there with that small amount of money. I personally find Cabernet Sauvignon, Burgundy, Chiani, and Nero d'Avola amongst the tastiest.

Spices

A comparatively concise list. Below is a list of spices used in Mediterranean cooking, listed in no order, in particular, to give that food the authentic taste you want. If you're a fan of this diet, it's worth it to buy many of these in bulk as you'll be using them a lot.

- Oregano
- Garlic
- Rosemary
- Thyme
- Marjoram
- Savory
- Crushed chili pepper
- Fennel
- Anise
- Basil
- Saffron
- Coriander (cilantro) and coriander seed
- Curley/Italian Parsley

Chapter 4: Eating Out

A night on the town is a past time everyone can get behind, and thankfully, on the Mediterranean diet, getting sloshed and talking that special someone who was giving you "the look" is very possible. (They're probably not giving you "the look" though.)

There are two things to consider when eating out and following a strict diet, the second question follows the first and can be further broken into component pieces.

The first is: How do I eat? Not so much "where," as a quick phone call and some basic internet research can tell you about the cuisine of the restaurant in question. Rather, what should I keep in mind when eating at particular restaurants, chains, delis, food trucks, kiosks, shacks, whatever. The second is a question which assumes that you're not being too zealous in times of going out - "How strict do I want to be?" Unfortunately, that's a much more complicated question – that's up to you. That depends on your diet goals, what the restaurant serves, your activity level, and all sorts of other things we'll talk about later. As for now, we'll just get into some basics of the "how" when it comes to eating out.

1. Know your restaurant and its menu

Try to pick a restaurant that fits your diet. Badger your friends loudly, consider buying an air horn to blow when they suggest other restaurants. If this doesn't work, prepare accordingly.

If you know that the place you're going to isn't going to have the food you want, it might be necessary to have a meal beforehand. If you're worried about anything, remember to ask the waiter for their menu's nutritional content.

2. Consider carrying "supplemental" nutrition

This may seem a little odd but stick with me. The greatest minds were never deterred by the looks the crowd gave them. If all the salads are smothered with ranch or sugary "Italian" dressing, that's where your trusty flask/bottles of olive oil and red wine vinegar come in.

3. Eat at restaurants that follow your diet plan

A simple enough idea, right? While many restaurants may claim to have true Mediterranean options, they can often be lacking, cut corners, or just have a paltry selection. Cuisines that are considered Mediterranean are the following: Spanish, Greek, Italian, Egyptian, Turkish, Lebanese, Jewish, Moroccan, Tunisian, Algerian, and Arabic, so look for an eatery with a wait staff who barely speaks English.

4. Try not to go too nuts on the white bread

Many restaurants will serve some form of white bread as an accompaniment with meals, usually with butter. These are high-calorie foods that both certainly have a place in the diet, but, for the most part, should be eaten sparingly. If there's an option for a whole grain option, it's better to take that or opt out of it altogether.

5. Avoid deep-fried foods

Some of the most popular appetizers and entrees for many people are things like breaded and fried wings, cheese, or something following that general principle. These foods are usually always fried in lower-quality oil, and the breading is plain, not good for you no matter how you slice it. Depending on where you're eating, there are probably ways to replace what might give your heart some problems 20 years down the line – such as a salad, or steamed, grilled, or at the very least – unbreaded - option of the same plate.

6. Sharing is caring

If everyone needs a bit of warm up, split an appetizer between at least three people to keep your calorie count down.

7. When you order meat, try to find out what kind

Different cuts of meat vary massively in their fat and protein content, and if you're looking to stay relatively lean, try to find out what parts of the animal they use. Chicken breast and pork loin and tenderloin will always be very lean.

8. Find out what kind of oil is used

One of the main purposes of this diet is that in taking an amount of olive oil, in any sort of sauce or dish, find out what the main cooking oil used was. Ask them to substitute it for olive oil if it doesn't match your current needs. Avoid too much cream, vegetable oil, and butter.

9. Always try to get your vegetables in

Try to eat vegetables either as a side or in the dish. The Mediterranean diet is very high in vegetables, and try to think how this dish would have been made if it was being crafted in that environment. It would either come with a bunch of vegetables cooked and with it, or a bunch served with a side salad or steamed vegetables of some breed.

10. Salad protocol

Many establishments serve a dressing of high-fat and high sugar, usually of low-quality fat. If you weren't brave enough to bring in your own olive oil and vinegar, control how much dressing you use by dipping your fork into and then eating your salad. It will greatly cut down on the amount you end up using.

11. Don't overeat because you paid for it

If you feel done, you're done – simple as that. No need to push on farther into the unventured gastric territory and risk bloat and discomfort. A very simple diet maxim that is often not employed is "don't eat until you're full, eat until you're not hungry." Simple, amazing, and seemingly common sense. But most people might be tempted to finish a meal they order in a restaurant simply because they spent money on it, but instead, pack it up, take it home, call a waiter as soon as you're done with it so you're not picking at it throughout the night like an indecisive chicken. Make eating at that restaurant worth two meals instead of one, and therefore, an almost-justifiable dietary and financial offense.

12. Have a coffee after dinner instead of dessert

The Italian course for meals is obnoxiously long and complicated; an aperitif to get you ready to eat, antipasto, pasta, main course, fruit and cheese, dessert and coffee, and digestif, a drink made to aid in digestion. Streamline this process, take inspiration from it without living it to keep yourself lighter, and just have a single shot of espresso if it's available, unadorned, no cream or sugar. It'll help suppress your appetite so you won't be hungry later or tempted to order a sugar-bomb dessert dish.

13. If dessert is inevitable...

If the sweet and decadent bounty of 4 blueberries and an apple slice isn't enough to satiate your sweet tooth, keep dessert under control. Order a single dessert for the whole table, and remember to keep mindfulness in mind when doing so, and only have a few bites, but make them the best bites of dessert you've ever had.

14. If you want to get loose...

Drinks are often the natural conclusion to dinner, and if you want to get a little twisted, start with wine, but don't finish with it. A glass or two has some well-regarded health benefits, but the carbohydrate count from it quickly adds up. Instead, stick to the harder stuff. Clear, unflavored liquor with seltzer is a good choice. All calories from the alcohol – the thing you're actually trying to feel, and none of the extra calories of sugar or carbohydrates.

15. Make sure you have a good support group

While everyone has a friend who can somehow vacuum up a box of dry pasta a night along with a pound of steak and a butter-pudding smoothie (for a first course, of course!) we're not all like that. Some of us have to watch what we eat lest the reaper comes creeping around the corner guised in obesity and diabetes come to harvest our essence and bring us back to where we came. In cases where you're really trying to stick to your diet, this is where it pays to have a social circle that will support you through it and not incessantly teases you about your new goals and restrictions. Try to avoid hanging out with the first guy as well, as seeing temptation will beat down resolve. Make sure they know why you're doing it, so they can support you when you go out, by either agreeing to whatever two restaurants in town you can eat at, or just by encouraging you when you're tempted, and by using one of our most ancient techniques for behavior control – in-group shaming, when you fall down.

How strict do I have to be?

Managing cravings is a big part of being on a diet, and for many people, it can be the hardest part, too. While changing what you eat on a day-to-day basis is one thing, when social pressures are mixed in, and possibly alcohol, inhibitions lower. There's a reason why the phenomena of "peer pressure" exists – because it's a powerful tool in modulating behavior. Seeing your friends binge and eat five desserts each will make you want to do it, too. This is probably a big reason why diets fail. You aren't sure what's appropriate and what's not, and in what quantities. The answer to how strict to be when you go out is in no way an easy one and is controlled by dozens of different factors in your life. The second half of this chapter is about knowing when you can get a little loose with your eating, and when you should reel it in, and ways to avoid temptations and keep yourself under control.

Remember back at the beginning of the book? We had talked about your goals - why are you on this diet, what do you hope to accomplish? Weight loss, reducing the chance of a disease, athletic performance? Think of where you are right now, where you want to be, and how close you are. Your genes and past behavior also play a huge role. If your older relatives look at a piece of cake and gain a pound, the same biology is probably present in you. Past behavior as well – are you prone to binging or can you control yourself? Psychologically stable people usually have an easier time controlling themselves, so making sure that you don't use food as an emotional crutch is a big aspect. Finally, there's your activity level – while fit people generally have greater discipline, they also have a little more wiggle room when it comes to indulgences, as long as it's not happening every night.

Goals

Let's get one thing straightened out right now. If weight loss is your primary goal, there really is no way around the simple and firm tenet that indulging will set you back, no matter how infrequently. This does mean never indulge, the opposite in fact. Some indulgences are good for you, because if you continually refuse the idea of it, and one day you break, you break that much worse. It's better to go out with your friends and have a few drinks and journey outside your dietary zone a few times a month than it is to save it all up in one session and binge drink and eat. Binge drinking and eating is shocking to the body and can result in serious long-term damage if you're not careful. An occasional indulgence will help curb your appetite for them in the long run – they'll seem like special treats as opposed to dire and gnawing needs.

Say your goal is something a little more unconventional, at least when dieting is concerned. Say you're trying to put on weight for a sport you play because you're not strong enough or need to change weight classes. If you've been following and maintaining your diet very well so far, a little indulgence may actually do you some good, because the extra calories would help fuel the recovery you so desperately need to change your body composition. Of course, considering what to order is important too – this is not an excuse to bulk up on ice cream, but usually, restaurant food is richer than what we're used to eating at home, but skimping on alcohol is recommended as alcohol can interfere with recovery, resting, and synthesis of new muscle tissue. Activity level and having a higher muscle mass will inherently raise your need for more calories in the first place, with people with a higher muscle mass having a higher basal metabolic rate – the calories you burn just existing – than an untrained person.

Lastly, if you're being called out on the town and you're mostly looking to avoid certain diseases, this is where some research needs to get done. It depends on what you think you might be prone to – heart disease would necessitate that you avoid any saturated fat when you go out, and especially trans fat. Diabetes might mean you've got to skip on dessert. One of the few uniting factors of all these sorts of different lifestyle diseases is inflammation, though. If you eat a diet that is prone to reducing it, it will help you across the board with avoiding things like heart disease, cancer, and diabetes. For considerations of anti-inflammatory foods, think some of the most common food in the diet – leafy green vegetables and fish. Try to find those on the diet, and remember to ask where the fish is from!

Genetics

This is one of the more grim realities of the world – that our genes control much of our health, from our bones to our heart to our metabolism. Some realities are simply impossible to avoid. It may be your family carries extra weight, and always has as far back as you can see, or that your blood sugar may spike unusually high, or you're prone to this or that health problem. Maybe it's the opposite, maybe your natural basal metabolic rate is so high that you can effectively be attached to a feeding tube and gain to no weight, though this is rarely a gift unaccompanied, there is always a price to pay.

Find out what runs in your family, what your health risks are. Alcoholism follows a notoriously sanguineous path, so avoiding drunken shenanigans may be in your best interest if so. If you know you're predisposed to gaining weight, drink water and try to vicariously live through your friends, as anything else carries the risk of extra inches around your waistline.

Past Behavior

Maybe, this is the best indicator of where you should draw the line when going out. Past behavior is among the top predictors of future behavior – if you've done it before, you'll do it again, and this is where it pays off to know who you really are. Be honest with yourself – if you know that you're capable of blacking out and eating an entire cake without tasting it, avoid the damn cake. Know what you use to comfort you. In the mindfulness section, I mentioned that you need to keep your relationship with food in mind. Make sure you don't use it as a replacement for affection and affirmation from yourself or any others.

Techniques to keep faith

It's the easiest thing in the world to preach what to do and what not to do, but it's a million times harder to actually do it. Thankfully, behavioral psychology was devised for this exact reason, and there is a slew of mental techniques to retrain your brain in times of weakness.

- **Visualization:** Take advantage of your unique human neurology and really reflect on the long-term consequences of your behavior. What will be the effects of binging with your friends in 5 years; financially, psychologically, socially and physically? Are you capable of living with this future you might create for yourself?
- **Honesty:** This really goes along with the content earlier in this chapter. Don't deny that you're on the diet to lose weight, or that you once drank an entire gallon of wine with a pound of crackers when you were sad. Lying to yourself is a way to rationalize behaviors you know you shouldn't be doing in the first place, and only takes you farther back. Also, ask yourself, is it really worth the splurging?
- **Stay informed:** Know your diet, know your health benefits. Simple things like knowing what you're putting in your body – provided you have the proper nutrition facts and all that, will greatly impact your mind.

- **Make a promise, out loud:** As we said before, in-group shaming is probably one of the most ancient ways we got people to do things we didn't like them doing. Make a point of telling everyone, as you go out, the things you plan to do or not to do. If you violate what you say, everyone can mock you for it, which is an awful feeling. Shame weighs heavier than a lead shawl on your shoulders.

- **Make a plan:** Elaborate on what you intend to do on that night you go out with writing. Make a promise to yourself that you won't go crazy, or that you'll enjoy within reason. Writing down things like that can help dispel anxieties about the night and keep you sharp and focused.

Eating out the Mediterranean

Overall, eating out on the Mediterranean diet is not challenging, as long as you keep some basic dieting strategies in mind. The diet is not dogmatically restrictive, but it's still recommended to keep some basic nutritional principles and eating strategies in mind when going out to avoid excess empty calories. (I'm looking at you, salad dressing). If you're going to go out and you're thinking of indulging, it's important to know when and how much, and strategies for figuring this out, before you do.

Chapter 5: Recipes

And here we are at the fun part – the actual food and what to eat. The recipes will be divided into some basic sections – "mother" recipes, a few basic fundamentals, and then breakfast, lunch, and dinner.

Mother Recipes

There are five things that can be made at home relatively easily that will save you a lot of money in the long run if you want to follow this diet Those five things are a bread, yogurt, a basic tomato sauce, bone stock, and tzatziki sauce.

Basic Yogurt

(110 kcal, P: 9 gr, Net Carbs: 12 gr, F: 3 gr for six ounces)

This might be your first time fermenting something, and that's fine. All it takes is some patience and a candy thermometer.

Equipment:

- Candy thermometer
- Stockpot
- Wooden spoon
- Measuring cup

Ingredients:

- Yogurt culture (Usually, a tablespoon or .5 cup of yogurt is fine)
- Milk (whole milk yogurt used for reference.)

Directions:

1. In the pot, pour your milk in. Yogurt and milk are a 1:1 ratio – a half gallon of milk makes a half gallon of yogurt. Attach your candy thermometer to the side of the pan and make sure it's immersed in the milk.
2. Gently raise the milk to 200 degrees Fahrenheit, while stirring the entire time. Make sure nothing gets stuck to the bottom and no skin forms on top. If it does, peel it off

or break it up into small pieces and mix it back up with the milk.

3. When the milk reaches 200 degrees, turn off the heat and take a half cup of it out in a measuring cup and mix it with the yogurt culture.

4. Then, mix the yogurt-milk mixture back into the warm milk.

5. Cover and store overnight. If you did it right, you should be met with the enzymatic smell of yogurt.

Recipe ideas:

1. Use as a marinade, sauce thickener, or by itself with oats and fruit.

2. Strain with cheesecloth to make into Greek yogurt.

Basic Focaccia Bread

(250 kcal, P: 9, Net Carbs: 36, F: 8, Fi: 2)

Making bread can be intimidating, but it's far easier than it looks. This recipe is almost foolproof, and it's extremely versatile. Just because it's called focaccia doesn't mean it has to be used in Italian food. It's a very simple crusty white bread that goes with many foods and can be seasoned however you want.

Equipment:

- Mixing bowl
- Baking pan

Ingredients:

- 1.5 cups of warm water (around 110 degrees, a bit hotter than your finger)
- 2.5 cups of flour
- .25 ounce of active-dry yeast
- Teaspoon of honey
- Salt and pepper to taste
- Any seasonings you want
- .25 cup of extra-virgin olive oil

Directions:

1. Dissolve your yeast into your water and stir.

2. Pour in your flour, oil, honey, salt, and pepper into your bowl with your water.

3. Mix until you have a warm, soft-but-not-sticky glob.

4. Cover with towel. Leave it in a warm place for an hour or so.

5. If you did it right, it will have risen and swelled up.

6. Take the ball of risen dough and roll it out onto your baking pan, season how you want.

7. Bake at 400 degrees Fahrenheit for 25 minutes or until golden brown

Basic Tomato sauce

(70 kcal, P: 3 gr, Net Carbs: 16 gr, F: 4 gr, Fi: 4 gr per cup.)

This can be used for pasta, eggs, bread, stews, soups, meats, beans – essentially anything savory you can think of. Its seasoning blend are endemic to the entire Mediterranean, so you can use it no matter what sort of cuisine you're making.

Equipment:

- Stainless steel pot
- Cutting board
- Knife
- Spoon

Ingredients:

- Salt and pepper
- 2 tablespoons extra-virgin olive oil
- Oregano
- 1 clove of garlic
- 1 teaspoon of honey
- 32 ounce can of crushed tomatoes

Directions:

1. Heat oil on medium-low heat and cut garlic. Add to pan when it gets warm.
2. After garlic has browned, add crushed tomatoes, salt, pepper, and oregano to taste, and a spot of honey.

3. Let it simmer for 30 minutes.

Recipe ideas:

1. Try eating it with eggs for Mediterranean style fried eggs, known under many different names.
2. It's great with toasted, browned sardines as a dip or a cooking liquid.

Basic Bone Stock

(Nutrition varies by batch)

This is the basis of many good soups and stews. Bone stock can be made from any animal, pig, chicken, or beef, but the most common are pork and chicken. You can usually find cuts of the beef femur to be used as stock, but pork ribs and chicken skeletons also work great. If you want an extra-rich version, use something like chicken feet or pork trotters. The gelatin leeches out, lending extra body and flavor. If the fat suspended in the broth puts you off, you can put it in the fridge and wait for it to rise to the top. Then, you can simply peel it off.

Equipment:

- Stockpot
- Roasting pan
- Knife
- Cutting board

Ingredients:

- Salt and pepper
- 1 Tablespoon of olive oil
- 1 clove of garlic
- 1 onion
- 2 ribs of celery
- 3 lb of bones

Directions:

1. Preheat oven to 350.
2. Slice vegetables finely, arrange them and the bones on the roasting tray, pour oil and sprinkle with salt and pepper.
3. Roast for 40-50 minutes until browned.
4. Remove pan from oven.
5. Take bones and vegetables and put them in a Stockpot. Fill it with water until covered.
6. Bring to rolling boil, and then reduce to a simmer.
7. Let it simmer for 12-24 hours.

Tzatziki Sauce

(250 kcal, P: 18 gr, Net Carbs: 6 gr, F: 17 gr per 7 ounces)

The tangy sauce they put on your gyro and used as a dipping sauce in much of the eastern Mediterranean for things like falafel and gyro meat. It is very easy to make at home, and cucumber can be added for additional freshness

Equipment:

- Mixing bowl
- Cutting board
- Knife

Ingredients

- .5 tablespoon of extra-virgin olive oil
- 7 ounces of whole fat Greek yogurt
- 1 clove of garlic
- Juice of .25 a lemon
- Dill

Directions:

1. Chop your garlic and dill fincly.
2. Add yogurt, dill, olive oil, garlic, and lemon juice to the bowl. Cover.
3. Let sit overnight. Flavors are enhanced by doing so.

Breakfast

This is the most important meal of the day, as wisdom decrees. Mediterranean diets tend to have simple breakfasts of just bread, oil, and a light protein, and many of these aren't codified here because of their simplicity. This obviously changes depending on personal preference, country, and, of course, hunger and skill level.

Mediterranean toast

(535 kcal, P: 16 gr, Net Carbs: 56 gr, F: 28 gr, Fi: 5 gr)

This is a simple and hearty meal composed of foods from across the Mediterranean.

Equipment:

- Toaster
- Cutting board
- Knife

Ingredients:

- Salt and pepper
- 5 olives
- Tomato

- 1 tablespoon of olive oil
- 1 boiled egg
- Half Ciabatta roll

Directions:

1. Slice egg into pieces, tomato in slices, and olives bisected.
2. Toast the bread until it looks nice and golden.
3. Pour oil over the bread slice, and top with egg, olives, tomatoes, and salt and pepper.

Fisherman's Eggs

(410 kcal, P: 41 gr, F: 26 gr)

A hearty breakfast from those men who worked the docks, this breakfast is full of healthy fats, omega-3s, and protein to get you through the day.

Equipment:

- Spatula
- Cast iron pan
- Cutting board
- Knife

Ingredients:

- 1 clove of garlic
- 1 tablespoon of extra-virgin olive oil
- 1 can of sardines packed in olive oil
- 3 eggs

Directions:

1. Preheat oven to broil.
2. Heat the oil on a pan at medium-low. Meanwhile, smash and dice the garlic.
3. Once the oil is shiny, add garlic to the pan along with the drained can of sardines. Break them up and brown them.
4. Once the oven is heated, broil for 4 minutes.

5. Take the pan out of the oven, crack your three eggs in and stick her back in for three minutes.
6. Take out, scoop it off the pan, and serve on focaccia bread.

Eggs in Purgatory

(250 kcal, P: 20 gr, Net Carbs: 7 gr, F: 15 gr, Fi: 2 gr)

A classic Italian dish that can be changed into the classic Moroccan version, with just the addition of some onion, chili, feta, and paprika.

Equipment:

- Pan with cover
- Cutting board (For shakshuka)
- Knife (Shakshuka)

Ingredients:

- 1 tablespoon of extra-virgin olive oil
- .5 cups of tomato sauce (See "mother" recipes)
- 3 eggs

Directions:

1. Heat sauce in a pan until bubbling, keep covered.
2. Make small wells in the sauce for the eggs. Add olive oil on the exposed parts.
3. Crack the eggs into the oil in the pan with the sauce.
4. Cover, turn heat to low and let poach for 5-8 minutes.

To make shakshuka:

1. Heat oil in a pan and finely dice the onion.

2. Add onion and chili flakes to the pan, mix in the tomato sauce.
3. Add a pinch of paprika.
4. After the eggs are poached, add feta cheese and serve.

Breakfast Salad

(180 kcal, P: 5 gr, Net Carbs: 8 gr, F: 10 gr, Fi: 2 gr per cup)

This is something like a milder version of a Greek salad, the same thing, but without the feta cheese and oregano, and with added spinach. This is a great healthy beginning to the day.

Equipment:

- Mixing bowl
- Spoon and fork
- Cutting board
- Knife

Ingredients:

- Salt and pepper
- Tablespoon of extra virgin olive oil and red wine vinegar
- 1 cucumber
- 1 tomato
- .5 cup of spinach

Directions:

1. Slice your cucumber in little coins, and cut them in half. Cut your tomatoes into quarters, and your spinach as fine as you can get it.
2. Throw these in your mixing bowl, dress with oil and vinegar, and season with salt and pepper.

3. Throw it in the fridge overnight to let the flavors really incorporate.

Breakfast Frittata

(200 kcal, P: 10 gr, Net carbs: 10 gr, F: 12 gr, Fi: 2 gr per slice)

A frittata is a savory Italian egg-based casserole usually with vegetables, cheese, and meat. This a version featuring an energy rush for those busy mornings, but still with plenty of protein and healthy fat.

Equipment:

- Cast iron pan
- Spatula
- Cutting board
- Knife
- Whisk
- Bowl

Ingredients:

- Salt and pepper
- 1 clove of garlic
- 2 red potatoes
- Bundle of green onion
- Cheese for grating
- 6 eggs

Directions:

1. Preheat oven to 350.

2. Heat the oil the pan. Mince your garlic and green onions and potatoes. Fry the potatoes first until golden brown, and then add your garlic and onions.
3. Crack your eggs into a bowl while whisking and grating some cheese and adding the salt and pepper and oregano.
4. Once the vegetables are cooked, add eggs to the pan, and put uncovered in the oven until eggs are firm.

Overnight Greek Oatmeal

(220 kcal, P: 9 gr, Net Carbs: 60 gr, F: 5 gr, and Fi: 7 gr)

There's an old quote about oatmeal; "Oats. A grain, which in England is generally given to horses, but in Scotland supports the people." I'm not sure if Greeks eat oatmeal. It always seemed like more of a northern European staple, but this fiber and energy-rich meal takes inspiration from their cuisine.

Equipment:

- Bowl
- Knife
- Cutting board
- Refrigerator

Ingredients:

- .3 cup of milk
- Pinch of cinnamon
- 3 dried figs
- Teaspoon of honey
- 3 dried dates
- .5 cups of oatmeal

Directions:

1. Chop your dried fruit into bits, set aside.
2. Combine your milk, splash of honey, fruit, and oatmeal, and mix thoroughly.

3. Throw it in the fridge for at least 8 hours.

4. When you open the fridge, it should be a solidified, semi-sweet, and rich porridge.

Lunch

Lunches are usually light and casual affairs in this corner of the world, a quick break from work to refuel before getting back to whatever labor you were involved with. This is where pasta comes in – as it's easy to digest and quick to get down and provides you with a rush of energy. The diet's most questionable components, charcuterie, eaten for centuries also act as a protein of the poor.

Pasta with Chili, Garlic, and Oil

(320 kcal, P: 7 gr, Net Carbs: 40 gr, F: 15 gr, Fi: 2 gr per cup)

Called "Pasta aglio e olio" in Italian - the most common pasta dish in Italy because of its taste and simplicity. Think of it as the Mediterranean equivalent to instant Ramen.

Equipment:

- Cutting board
- Knife
- Pot

Ingredients:

- Pasta (Spaghetti or other long pasta preferred)
- 1 garlic clove
- 1 tablespoon of olive oil

- Chili flakes

Directions:

1. Heat oil on medium-low. Meanwhile, smash garlic and cut fine.
2. Add chili to the oil once it's heated, then add your garlic clove. When your garlic is fragrant and lightly brown, it's done
3. Meanwhile, boil your pasta until al dente. Tender but not soft.
4. Strain the pasta, add back to the pot, and toss with garlic, oil, and chili.
5. Serve with either shredded parmesan or Romano cheese or Italian flat leaf parsley.

Mediterranean Stuffed Chicken

(300 kcal, P: 43 gr, Net Carbs: 10 gr, F: 14 gr, Fi: 4 gr per breast)

This is chicken cordon bleu's thinner, more fibrous cousin. Not of any country in particular, but a mishmash of different flavors and textures.

Equipment:

- Frying pan
- Cutting board
- Knife
- Roasting pan
- Meat tenderizer

Ingredients:

- Salt and pepper
- Oregano
- 2 tablespoons extra virgin olive oil
- Chicken breast
- 1 Tomato
- 1 Zucchini
- 10 Black olives
- Red onion
- Feta cheese

Directions:

1. Preheat oven to 350 degrees Fahrenheit.

2. Butterfly the chicken breast and separate. Pound it as flat as you can with the tenderizer, set aside.

3. Finely slice all your vegetables in long, thin pieces. Divide your olives into fourths.

4. On your tenderized chicken, make slices against the grain and tuck your vegetables in. Season with salt, pepper, and oregano.

5. Heat olive oil in a pan of medium size.

6. Brown chicken briefly in the pan.

7. Take out of the pan. Put on a roasting pan and sprinkle with feta cheese.

8. Toss it in the oven, come back in 25 minutes.

9. Take out of oven, rest, and enjoy.

Tortellini in broth with kale

(210 calories, P: 11 gr, Net Carbs: 33 gr, F: 5 gr, and Fi: 3 gr per 2 cups)

A famous soup from the north of Italy, and can be made extra delicious by using the recipe for the broth in the first section. It is comforting and warming on a winter's day, but also light enough to be enjoyed on-the-go.

Equipment:

- Cutting board
- Knife
- Pan

Ingredients:

- 1 tablespoon olive oil
- Oregano
- Rosemary
- Flat-leaf parsley
- Bundle of kale
- 1 onion
- 1 clove of garlic
- 1 lb of tortellini
- Bone stock

Directions:

1. Heat olive oil on medium-low in the pan.

2. Smash and dice the garlic into fine pieces and dice onion finely.
3. Add onion, garlic, and rosemary to a pan, sweat until golden brown.
4. Add the stock and bring to a boil.
5. Boil the tortellini until al dente, and then add the oregano.
6. 2 or 3 minutes before the tortellini is finished, rip up the kale and parsley and let them boil in soup. When everything is soft and the tortellini rises to the top, the soup is complete.

Tunisian Eggplant Salad

(290 kcal, P: 5 gr, Net Carbs: 12 gr, F: 24 gr, Fi: 5 gr per cup)

This is a recipe with probably a thousand variations around the Mediterranean, usually served cold or at room temperature with crusty bread. The eggplant absorbs the flavor of the oil and tomato very well, making this a decadent but guilt-free treat. It's sweet and sour and a good side or main course.

Equipment:

- Can opener
- Cutting board
- Knife
- Pot
- Colander

Ingredients:

- Salt and pepper
- 2 tablespoons of red wine vinegar
- 1 teaspoon of honey
- 3 Tablespoons of extra-virgin olive oil
- 1 onion
- 2 cloves of garlic
- 1 Eggplant
- 2 bell peppers
- Oregano

- 5 sage leaves
- Can of tomatoes, 15.5 ounces

Directions:

1. Heat oil in the pan to medium-low.
2. Slice the eggplant into discs and salt, put in a colander. (This keeps the eggplant from drinking up too much oil)
3. Slice the onions and garlic.
4. Add the onions and garlic to the pan.
5. Remove from the pan.
6. Slice the bell peppers into strips and add to the pan.
7. Remove from the pan once softened.
8. After 0.5 hours have passed, take the eggplant from the strainer and sauté in pan until soft.
9. Add tomatoes, onions, garlic, peppers, herbs, vinegar, and honey. Simmer until thickened.
10. Refrigerate overnight, serve cold.

Pasta alla Norma

(320 kcal, P: 9 gr, Net Carbs: 49 gr, F: 10 gr, Fi: 5 gr per cup)

This is one of the national dishes of the island of Sicily – said to have been inspired by writer Nino Martoglio – who compared its delicate taste to the opera Norma, by Vincenzo Bellini.

Equipment:

- Cutting board
- Knife
- Pot
- Colander

Ingredients

- Salt and pepper
- 3 tablespoons extra-virgin olive oil
- 5 basil leaves
- Ricotta salata, parmesan, or pecorino romano
- 8oz of pasta – rigatoni works best.
- 1 eggplant
- 2 cups of tomato sauce

Directions:

1. Slice eggplant into discs, salt, and put in a colander to prevent it from drinking up too much oil.
2. After the time has passed, heat the oil in a pan of medium size. Add the eggplant and cook until soft.

3. Add tomato sauce to the eggplant and simmer until eggplant is tender.
4. Meanwhile, boil the water for the pasta and cook until it is al dente.
5. Just before serving, tear up basil leaves and add to the sauce pot.
6. Take pasta, dress with sauce, and grate some ricotta salata or other hard cheese on top.

Stuffed Pita

(295 kcal, P: 18 gr, Net Carbs: 33 gr, F: 13 gr, Fi: 14 gr per whole pita)

A quick bite you can take with you on-the-go, this little pocket of nutrition supplies everything you need to keep you alert and focused so you aren't yelled at by your boss for passing out at work!

Equipment:

- Cutting board
- Knife
- **Ingredients**
- Juice of .25 lemon
- 1 Tomato
- .25 red onion
- 4 tablespoons of hummus
- .5 cups of spinach
- Boiled egg
- 2 oz crumble of feta cheese
- Whole pita

Directions:

1. Finely chop your onion, chop your tomato in slices, and cut your boiled egg into quarters
2. Open up your pita bread. Smear your hummus on both sides to work as a kind of "food glue."

3. Lay your spinach, then the tomato down, and top with your boiled egg quarters to weigh everything down.
4. Squeeze your lemon juice over it and lay your feta cheese on top and enjoy.

Greek Salad

(180 kcal, P: 5 gr, Net Carbs: 8 gr, F: 10 gr, Fi: 2 gr per 160 grams)

The original greenless salad – the Salad that kept the men of Athens fighting Persia. It's delicious!

Equipment:

- Cutting board
- Knife
- Mixing Bowl

Ingredients

- Salt and pepper
- Savory
- Oregano
- 1 tablespoon of extra-virgin olive oil
- 1 tablespoon red wine vinegar
- cucumber
- Tomato
- .5 red onion
- 4 ounces of feta cheese

Directions:

1. Cut your cucumber into disks, tomato into fourths, and finely dice your onion.
2. Mix your oil and vinegar together.

3. Toss all your vegetables together. Pour your dressing over it. Season with oregano and savory, and crumble up your feta cheese on top of it.

Roasted chickpeas

(255 kcal, P: 15 gr, Net Carbs: 47 gr, F: 1 gr, Fi: 11 gr)

Perfect for either a light lunch or a snack, these can be eaten with yogurt sauce (tzatziki) or with greens and rice.

Equipment:

- Cutting board
- Pot
- Knife
- Roasting pan

Ingredients

- 1 tablespoon extra-virgin olive oil
- Salt and pepper
- Onion
- .5 cup of dry chickpeas soaked for 8 hours or overnight
- Water or stock

Directions:

1. Heat olive oil on medium low.
2. Finely dice your onion and garlic, adding to the pan when the oil is hot.
3. Cook until brown, and then add your water or stock and chickpeas.
4. Simmer until the chickpeas are tender. Add salt and pepper.

5. Preheat oven to 350 degrees F.

6. Arrange the chickpeas with plenty of room on a roasting pan, and cook for 30 minutes or until crispy.

Calabrese Salad

(220 kcal, P: 13 gr, Net Carbs: 5 gr, F: 17 gr, Fi: 1 gr per cup)

This is another greenless salad, this time coming from the "toe" of Italy, Calabria. Famous for its richness of flavor and fullness of ingredients, Calabrese can be an awesome lunch on its own.

Equipment:

- Cutting board
- Knife

Ingredients

- Salt and pepper
- 1 tablespoon of extra-virgin olive oil
- 1 tablespoon balsamic vinegar
- .5 lb of mozzarella
- 1 tomato
- 10 basil leaves

Directions:

1. Cut your tomato and mozzarella into 0.25 of inch slices.
2. Arrange them on a plate: tomato, basil leaf, and mozzarella.
3. Drizzle the top with balsamic vinegar and olive oil. Season with salt and pepper to taste.

Mediterranean Wrap

(550 kcal, P: 34 gr, F: 22 gr, Net Carbs: 54 gr, Fi: 6 gr)

This is a modern invention with all the components of a good Mediterranean diet, from fibrous bread to lean protein to fresh vegetables. Carry one of these around with you and annoy everyone who asks how your burrito is by smugly responding you're having a Mediterranean wrap, THANK YOU VERY MUCH.

Equipment

- Knife
- Cutting board

Ingredients

- Salt and pepper
- .5 cup of chicken breast
- 2 ounces of feta cheese
- 1 tablespoon of hummus
- Juice of .25 lemon
- .5 of Cucumber
- .5 Tomato
- .25 Red onion
- .5 cups of spinach
- Tortilla wrap

Directions:

1. Finely dice your spinach and onion. Quarter your tomato, and cut your cucumber into discs.
2. Smear down your hummus, chopped vegetables, feta, and chicken into the tortilla and spray with lemon juice and season with salt and pepper.
3. Wrap like a burrito, pack up and eat.

Dinner

By necessity, dinners are hearty but not gut-destroying affairs in the Mediterranean. A day as a rural worker in this part of the world can be grueling, but the bounty of the earth will always provide them with enough energy to get up the next day and get their work done. Fish and chicken are common dinners, but occasionally, heavier roasts and stews are also not unknown.

Pesce alla Ghiotta - Glutton's Swordfish

(220 kcal, P: 28 gr, Net Carbs: 6 gr, F: 14 gr, Fi: 1 gr per 100 grams)

While the name of this recipe may have you thinking you'll be packing on a gut, glutton in this context is a bit more delicate. It means someone who enjoys all the best things in life – but not necessarily in excess. It's a dish that's great for impressing company as well, so it would be a sure-fire hit for the next dinner party.

Equipment:

- Pan
- Cutting board
- Knife

Ingredients (For three servings)

- 1 tablespoon extra-virgin olive oil
- 1 tablespoon extra-lite olive oil
- Salt and pepper
- Oregano
- Marjoram
- Capers
- Chili flakes
- 10 olives
- 1 onion
- 1.5 cups of tomato sauce
- 1 lb of swordfish

Directions:

1. Dice your olives and onion as fine as possible.
2. Turn your pan on medium-high and fill with extra-lite olive oil.
3. Season the swordfish with salt and pepper.
4. Brown the swordfish on both sides and remove from pan.
5. Lower heat on the pan and add extra-virgin olive oil.
6. Add onion, chili, and olives to the pan and sweat until golden brown.
7. Add tomato sauce, oregano, marjoram, capers, and swordfish and let them cook until the swordfish falls apart easily when stabbed with a fork.

Lemon Rosemary Roasted Chicken

(140 kcal, P: 14 gr, F: 9 gr for thigh meat; 366 kcal, P: 55 gr, F: 14 gr for breast) (180 kcal, P: 3 gr, F: 9 gr, Net Carbs: 23 gr, Fi: 3 gr for roasted vegetables)

Roasting a whole chicken can sometimes be something of an affair; or as I call it the 13th labor of Hercules. There's a decent amount of prep work involved but the results are usually worth it if everything goes as planned. The cut vegetables at the bottom work to keep the chicken from essentially boiling in its own juices.

Equipment:

- Cutting board
- Knife
- Mixing bowl
- Whisk
- Foil
- Roasting pan

Ingredients

- Salt
- Pepper
- Rosemary
- Juice of .5 lemon
- 2 red potatoes
- 1 carrot

- 1 onion
- 3 tablespoons of olive oil
- Whole chicken

Directions:

1. Preheat oven to 400.
2. Whisk together 2 tablespoons of oil, salt, pepper, lemon juice, and rosemary in a bowl.
3. Dice your vegetables into quarters, dressing with 1 tablespoon of olive oil, salt, pepper, and rosemary, and put in roasting pan.
4. Using a knife, separate chicken skin.
5. Pour oil under the skin of the chicken breast and leg.
6. Roast covered for 45 minutes.
7. Take it out, remove foil, and drop the heat to 350.
8. Put it back in for half an hour.
9. Take it out. If juice runs clear, it's cooked. If not, put it back in for 10 more minutes.
10. Let it rest for 15 minutes before carving, then serve.

Pasta con le Sarde

Pasta with sardines may not sound particularly appealing if your palate is not so adventurous. But if treated right, this little canned fished can be astoundingly tasty contributors to a dish. This Italian classic is full of omega-3s, protein, and calcium.

(710 kcal, P: 28 gr, Net Carbs: 72 gr, F: 33 gr per half cup)

Equipment:

- Cutting board
- Knife
- 2 Pans

Ingredients:

- Anchovy paste
- Salt and pepper
- Red pepper flakes
- .5 lb of spaghetti
- 1 onion
- 2 cloves garlic
- 4 tablespoons of extra-virgin olive oil
- .25 a cup of white wine
- 2 cans of sardines, drained
- .25 cup of pine nuts
- .5 cup of bread crumbs

Directions:

1. Heat oil in a pan on medium-low. Dice your garlic and onions and add to pan.

2. As they soften, add red pepper flakes, anchovy paste, and sardines. Cook until brown.

3. Toast breadcrumbs in oil in a separate pan, and then put aside.

4. Meanwhile, boil water for pasta, cook al-dente.

5. Add wine to pan contents, add pine nuts and cook down for 10 more minutes.

6. Turn heat off, spoon sauce together with pasta and add bread crumbs as a topper.

Greek Codfish

(200 kcal, P: 41 gr, F: 2 gr per 6 ounces)

This can be done either with salted, dried codfish that's been rehydrated or with a fresh cut. It's heavy on lemon and spices – the Greek way of doing things.

Equipment:

- Baking pan
- Knife
- Cutting board

Ingredients:

- 1 tablespoon extra-virgin olive oil
- Juice of .5 a lemon
- Salt and pepper
- Oregano
- Garlic powder
- Cumin
- .5 bundle Flat-leaf parsley
- 6-oz piece of codfish

Directions:

1. Preheat oven to 350.
2. Lay fish on a pan. Season with salt, pepper, half the lemon juice, parsley, cumin, garlic powder, and oregano.

3. Bake for 25 minutes or until crispy, taking out once at the 15-minute mark to pour the remaining lemon juice on.
4. Take fish out of the pan and let it rest for 10 minutes.

Oregano Pork Loin

(325 kcal, P: 45 gr, F: 15 gr)

Pork loin is one of the more "aristocratic" meats – but can still be purchased cheaply if you know where to look. It's lean and full of protein. Because of this, it tends to dry out when grilled. That's why we're doing a dry brine, the longer the better.

Equipment:

- Grill or broiler
- Roasting pan for broiler
- Grill tongs
- Meat Thermometer

Ingredients

- .25 cup of salt
- Pepper
- 1 tablespoon of extra-virgin olive oil
- .25 cup of sugar
- 6oz of pork loin
- Oregano

Directions:

1. Combine salt and sugar. Rub on pork with pepper and oregano and marinade for at least 8 hours. A day is best.
2. When ready to cook, get the grill heat to medium. Douse the loin piece with oil.

3. Grill, flipping once until the meat reads 160 degrees Fahrenheit. Check with a meat thermometer.

Tunisian-Style Salmon

(410 kcal, P: 40 gr, F: 27 gr per 7 ounces)

Tunisia has been the home of many great civilizations over the past thousand years, namely the Phoenicians, Carthaginians, and the Umayyad Caliphate. They've long been a trading port – a place where you could get anything if you knew where to look. This reflects in the complexities of this dish.

Equipment:

- Roasting pan
- Plastic bag
- Mortar and pestle or herb grinder

Ingredients

- Salt and pepper
- .5 cup of flour
- Juice of 2 lemons
- 2 saffron threads
- 1 clove of crushed garlic
- Paprika
- Oregano
- Cumin
- Savory
- 7 ounces salmon fillet
- 6 tablespoons of extra-virgin olive oil

Directions:

1. Grind saffron threads and dissolve in lemon juice.
2. Combine lemon juice, garlic, and olive oil in a bag with fish. Marinade for 8 hours or overnight.
3. Dredge the salmon in a mixture of salt and pepper, oregano, paprika, cumin, and savory.
4. Grill on 350, uncovered, until the fish flakes easily.

Fasolada – Greek White Bean Soup

(310 kcal, P: 11 gr, Net Carbs: 39 gr, F: 14 gr, Fi: 8 gr)

For the average Hellenic, a dish more like this was probably far more common. It is made from things that could be grown easily and eaten cheaply, but still hearty enough to keep your belly from rumbling in the dead of night.

Equipment:

- Pot
- Cutting board
- Knife

Ingredients:

- Bay leaf
- 1 cup of white dry beans, soaked overnight
- 1 clove of garlic
- Salt and pepper
- 3 tablespoon extra-virgin olive oil
- 2 carrots
- 2 ribs of celery
- Tablespoon of tomato paste
- 1 onion
- Water (or bone stock)
- Paprika

Directions:

1. Heat olive oil to medium-low heat.
2. Dice all vegetables and garlic and add to pan. Cook until aromatic and brown.
3. Deglaze the pan with water or stock, stirring in tomato paste and bay leaf.
4. Pour in beans and increase heat to boil.
5. Let simmer until beans swell and are soft enough to eat.

Spanish-Style Chicken Fricassee

(350 kcal, P: 30 gr, Net Carbs: 15 gr, F: 14gr, Fi: 4 gr per half cup)

Fricassee is a style of the dish with many different forms and countries of origin, sort of like how the name sounds neither 100% Spanish nor French. This particular version is enriched with beer – something not always commonly found in Mediterranean cuisine but is used to excellent and delicious effect.

Equipment:

- Pot
- Cutting board
- Knife

Ingredients:

- Salt and pepper
- Bay leaf
- 1 onion
- Cumin
- 1 clove of garlic
- Whole chicken, cut up
- 3 tablespoons of extra-virgin olive oil
- 2 tablespoons of extra-lite olive oil
- 1 bottle of light beer
- 2 cans of crushed tomatoes

- 6 red potatoes
- 12-ounce jar of Spanish olives

Directions:

1. Season the chicken parts with salt and pepper. Pour lite olive oil into the pan and put on medium high.
2. Brown all the chicken parts and set aside.
3. Lower the heat and add extra-virgin olive oil.
4. Dice the garlic, onion, and carrot finely and add to the oil. Cook until brown and fragrant.
5. Add tomatoes, beer, spices, potatoes, and chicken.
6. Boil for 2 to 3 hours, or until chicken falls apart with a fork.
7. Serve with rice.

Steak Pizzamaker's Style

(375 kcal, P: 36 gr, Net Carbs: 16 gr, F: 18 gr per 6 oz serving)

Pizzaiola – a pizzamaker in Naples, has a certain style of making a steak that is unusual, for most people, to say the least. Most people don't associate tomato sauce and steak, but this recipe melds the two excellently. This is best used with a tougher cut, like flank or brisket, but sirloin can serve just as well.

Equipment:

- 2 pans

Ingredients

- Salt and pepper
- 6 oz sirloin, flank, or brisket steak
- Oregano
- 1 tablespoon extra-lite olive oil
- 1 cup of tomato sauce

Directions:

1. Season your steak with salt, pepper, and oregano.
2. Meanwhile, get your tomato sauce simmering in the first pan.
3. Heat your extra-lite oil to high, and, when hot, sear your steak for 2 mins either side or until nicely browned.
4. Simmer in tomato sauce for 2-4 minutes and serve.

Stuffed Tomatoes

(450 kcal, P: 29 gr, Net Carbs: 30 gr, F: 24 gr, Fi: 5 gr per tomato)

Otherwise known in Turkish as Domates dolmasi – stuffed tomatoes are the rarer counterpart to the more often seen stuffed peppers, but equally delicious. Also enjoyed by the Greeks, these little flavor bombs have a reputation for being challenging, but all they take is a little patience and they can be made easily.

Equipment:

- Roasting pan
- Pot
- Frying pan
- Cutting board

Ingredients:

- 8 tomatoes
- Salt and pepper
- 1lb ground meat
- Oregano
- 1 cup of rice
- Sage
- Thyme
- Onion
- 1 clove of garlic

- .5 cup of tomato sauce
- 2 tablespoons extra-virgin olive oil

Directions:

1. Preheat oven to 350. Warm oil in a pan to medium-low.
2. Put rice on a boil, starting on high heat, and reducing to medium once it starts to boil over.
3. Finely dice the onions and garlic and fry in oil until brown.
4. Add meat, oregano, sage, and cook until the meat is browned.
5. Meanwhile, cut the top of tomato off and scoop out the guts.
6. Once the rice and meat is cooked, mix it together, and stuff it inside a tomato
7. Put tomatoes on baking sheet and pour tomato sauce on top of it.
8. Put tomato top back on top and bake for 25 minutes.

Chapter 6: Cultivation

Think of this as something like a little bonus to this book – and really, when you ponder over much of the material covered, it's no surprise that this would be an essential skill for those of us truly looking to dive into the diet as deeply as possible. This diet is one of the rural poor, who are farmers, by convention. These people always had fresh produce around the table, the star of many of their dishes, and they always knew how to grow their own food. This chapter only covers some of the basics, the easier vegetables, herbs, and fruits to grow, but hopefully, it's enough to get you started. You won't be milling your own flour or butchering your own cow, but at least you can taste your very own home-grown tomato, or at least stop having to buy basil at the grocery store every two weeks.

Herbs

Starting with an herb garden is inherently less threatening than trying to grow a vegetable – it's where most people start with gardening because you're basically just growing some tasty weeds and sticks, something even those of us with no gardening inclination can do.

Rosemary

"The Christmas herb," rosemary has a strong flavor and is extremely prevalent in many types of Mediterranean cuisine. It's not hard to grow, depending on where you live, and can soon grow to achieve the status of "obnoxious weed" if you're not too adamantly harvesting it.

There are two ways to grow rosemary – from seed or from a trimming. To get a quicker start, plant them indoors 9 weeks before your last frost. Once that's happened, plant them in well-drained, 70-degree soil with plenty of room to spread out, maybe three feet tall and three feet wide. When it flowers, trim it, and water enough to keep it moist but not swampy, maybe every other day. It needs full sun exposure to grow strong, and prune often to keep it from getting too skeletal. The younger the stems, the fresher the taste. They can be dried and used later.

Basil

A plant that must grow like a weed in the Mediterranean – but a plant that I often fail to plant and harvest here. It comes in many varieties, lemony lemon basil (creative name!) the anise-like taste of Thai, and the milder purple basil. Good for making pesto, calabrese, or enhancing the flavor of tomato sauce, basil likes heat to stay healthy.

When planting, it likes full sun and soil temperature in between 50 and 70 degrees. It needs the warmth to grow, with 8 hours of sun a day. Shove them into the ground a foot apart, and 0.25 of an inch deep. Same with rosemary – enough water is needed to keep it moist, but don't drown the plant. It should be drained regularly. When it flowers, trim to keep your plant producing leaves, but, as it's an annual, it will die in a year. So, toward the latter end of its lifespan, let the flower seed to get a new generation of plant.

Bonus: Their favorite neighbors are tomatoes, which is cute, as they go so well together.

Dill

Dill is a feathery-looking herb, commonly used in the eastern Mediterranean for soups and stews, and for pickling. It has the interesting effect of attracting certain helpful insects to your garden as well, predatory ones that drive off formican (ant) invaders and beetles. It also self-sows easily, so you can easily establish a permanent home for your herb.

Dill is also a full-sun plant. Interesting how all these Mediterranean plants need full sun! Keep the plants a foot and a half apart – and keep the soil warm, anywhere in the 60 to 70 degree-range. It does best when it's grown where it started. It does not tolerate transplanting and is somewhat frail – build a barrier so it's not knocked over by a strong wind. Water is best given every other day, and do not let flowers bloom on them. Within 20 to 30 days, some signs of dill should appear.

Thyme

Thyme is a great plant for both seasoning and using as a source of puns. It has an herbal flavor akin to oregano or marjoram, but in a warmer, less intense way. It's a great seasoning for milder soups and stews, usually with chickens or beans as a starring ingredient.

Thyme has a little more tolerance than the previous plants – you can plant it in the full or partial sun. It's cool with either, and it's a perennial, so it keeps coming back as long as you don't kill it. However, growing it from seeds can be a challenge. Try getting some from a friend in the form of clippings, and plant it 8 weeks before the last frost, and keeping the soil around 70 degrees. Keep it 8 inches away from its fellow sprigs, and water it every other day. Trim often and dry the sprigs in a dark area and store them airtight for continual use, or grind them into a powder.

Italian/Curly Parsley

A cousin to the dill plant with bright leaves, parsley is a common addition as both a flavoring agent and a decoration to Mediterranean cuisine. It is an absolute essential for any garden and great for health. It is full of micronutrients, fiber, vitamins, and minerals.

Like thyme, this breed of parsley enjoys both full sun and partial sun and warm weather, about 70 degrees Fahrenheit optimally. Plant seeds in their own pots, in their own homes 10 weeks before the last frost. Soaking the seeds overnight gets them to grow a little easier. She's a bit of a slow starter, so waiting 3 to 4 weeks may be required, but it can handle cold weather, so don't get discouraged if it's been awhile. If planting together, give 8 inches of space. If you need extra light, a grow lamp about 2 inches above gives the plants the stimulation needed. Water as needed. Check the soil often for dryness.

Wait until all three "heads" of the leaf are grown in before harvesting, but trim from the outer area. Leave the inner part to mature. To keep the stalks lively, put the stalks in water in the fridge. Drying parsley can sometimes reduce flavor.

Fruits and Vegetables

If you've managed to successfully grow a few of the things from the herb section, you're probably ready for a bigger challenge. Growing fresh produce can be intimidating, but give praise, we aren't working as sharecroppers, farmers, or, Zeus forbids, Neolithic agriculturalists. If we screw up, we can keep trying, – that's the key here, to keep trying. Growing vegetables can be frustrating to start with, but ultimately a very rewarding enterprise. We don't have the built-in knowledge of these farmer folks, but we have an infinite library of information to use at our leisure, so take advantage of it if there's something you want to grow.

Cucumber

A casual, easy to grow vegetable that loves the sun and water, cucumbers respond well to constant watering and climbs up space easily. They also grow quickly for vegetables, and in relative abundance, leaving you with more pickles than you know what to do with. They also grow in containers quite easily, making them an option even for those of us trapped in apartments.

Again, they like full sun, and soil around 70 degrees. Plant them inside earlier, then move two weeks after the last frost as they need the heat. The soil is better if it is a little alkaline, around 7 on the pH scale. Mix manure down 8 inches deep and ensure the soil is not too soggy. Plant the buds 3 to 5 feet apart and an inch deep. They need constant watering, one inch a week. Put your finger in the dirt, and if it's dry an inch down, water it. When sprouts emerge, increase water to a gallon a week. Harvest them before they're too big for optimal taste, and not yellow. Keep the plant picked to keep it producing.

Tomato

The perfect buddy to basil in the garden and the kitchen, a tomato is easy for the first time gardener. Tomatoes are also almost always better when picked fresh and local – supermarket tomatoes are known for being lighter on flavor and on nutrients. Consider pruning your plants earlier on for stronger-tasting fruits with a better taste, but fewer plants overall. They need lots of water and fertilizer in the form of eggshells or bone meal.

Start your tomatoes 6 to 8 weeks before the final frost to get them a good head start, and water them well to keep the roots healthy. They need full sun, and loose, well-drained soil. If doing them in pots, one tomato per pot. Cherry tomatoes grow exceptionally well in a pot. Keep your soil moist, and water it extra in a heat wave. It needs 6 to 8 hours a day of full sun for proper nourishment. Two inches of water a week to reach deep down into the roots, and trim leaves 12 inches below the stem. Leave them on the vine, let them ripen for as long as you can. If any fall off before that, let them finish in a paper bag. Don't refrigerate them either, keep them out in the open, and can be kept in a sealed plastic bag, frozen.

Zucchini

Zucchini is a famed vegetable because of their prolific nature – they keep producing and producing and producing several per day. That's why this is a good starter plant, it does good to encourage the beginning farmer. They taste similar to their yellow squash brethren, and are, in fact, simply their "winter squash" equivalent, and can be used in a similar way, for noodles or in roasts or stir-fries.

Start the seeds indoors, 3 weeks before the final cold snap of spring, with soil hovering around 60 degrees Fahrenheit. Planting it midsummer works well, too – you can avoid common pests and blights that happen earlier in the growing season. They need lots of compost and organic matter, egg shells, bone meal, that sort of thing, so make sure it's properly woven into the soil ahead of time. They like to be planted one-inch deep and about two feet apart, and regular, weekly watering down into the root system is needed. It is recommended to water them four inches down and keep adding more organic matter into the dirt for optimal growth.

Zucchini is best harvested early on when they're small and still tender to the touch for the best flavor. The larger the squash, the more the flavors "spread out," weakening them. They average two months to maturity, but once it gets going, you'll have enough to be sick of them. It's recommended to cut the vine instead of breaking it off.

Spinach

Popeye's favorite is full of iron, fiber, and vitamins A and K, and is also one of the easier and rewarding leaves to start with. It's best to start in the early spring but needs a fed, rich soil. Tilling in manure would be best for this, about a week before you plant, and the second the ground thaws, the seeds are ready to go in the ground. The quicker the seeding the better.

Spinach needs full sun exposure, but the soil should not rise above 70 degrees. Plant your seeds half an inch deep and cover, and one seed per inch. Water regularly, and don't be afraid if it gets cold. Spinach tolerates temperatures as low as 20 degrees Fahrenheit. As or harvesting – it's mostly by eye. When do you think they look best? Then they're best, don't wait too long, as bitterness will settle into it quickly after maturity. Cut it off at its base, from the outer plants in to give the inner plants more time to reach maturity.

Last words

Growing fruits, vegetables, and herbs is a rewarding hobby and an excellent addition to cooking and fits well with the protocol of the Mediterranean diet, but, it can be frustrating. As the beginning of the chapter said, start slow. Don't plant 10 different plants in 10 different ways and get frustrated and quit once they all die. Check them every day. Continual monitoring of their situation is the best way to asses their health and nip any problems in the bud before they start. Remember, too, that there are plenty of resources, from local gardeners and farmers in your area, to books, and the internet. Take advantage to maximize your growth potential, and to make your diet match its farmer origins as best it can.

Conclusion

The Mediterranean is a big place. Dozens of different cultures and languages and cuisines blending together, but this, and its lush climate are part of the reason why it's such a culinary powerhouse today. It's a bounty for both the soul and the body, fit for a peasant or an emperor. Hopefully, this book carried you to wherever you wanted to be – whether that was health, performance, or simple curiosity.

This book was not intended to be the be-all end-all publication on Mediterranean food, but it was structured to serve as a knowledge basis – to give you a complete idea of the most basics of where to look when it came to making choices for yourself. Just the essentials and then enough to get you started, with enough to carry you in confidence. Hopefully, that happened, I had a drachma for every time I wrote: "olive oil, wine, bread, fish, I'd be hegemon by now". We also tried to give you a solid, calorie-precise guide to what you'll be eating, not so you can obsessively track every calorie, but so you can start thinking about the food choices you make every day in hopes that it will encourage you to find your way to a healthy lifestyle.

Changing your diet isn't a simple thing, but hopefully, we provided enough examples to inspire you on a culinary journey. Hopefully, you've gone on to integrate some aspects of the diet, or maybe you've made the full switch, or maybe find a new recipe you might like or encourage you to see *how bad are sardines really?* Cooking and eating is a fundamental part of existence, and it is also one of the most rewarding for the body and spirit. At the very least, we have enriched your life in the smallest way. Enjoy your meals with your friends and family to best effect, and don't be afraid to plant a seed.

Whatever you've gleaned from this book, the one thing we must say is *Bon appetite!*

Made in the USA
San Bernardino, CA
04 May 2019